GROWING UP GREEN

Parents & Children Gardening Together

by
Alice Skelsey &
Gloria Huckaby

Illustration and photography by Norma Erler Rahn

WORKMAN PUBLISHING COMPANY NEW YORK

Cover design: Paul Hanson
Interior design, photographs and illustrations: Norma Erler Rahn
Typeset by Vermont Photo-Tape Services and printed by the George Banta Company

First printing November 1973

5 6 7 8 9 10

Plants on cover courtesy of The Plant Shed

Workman Publishing Company, 231 East 51st Street, New York, New York 10022.
Printed in the United States of America. ISBN: Hardbound—0-911104-22-4
Softbound—0-91110423-2

In memory of Anne Tipton Fulton,
who grew up green and free and shared it all with us

Love to our own green-growing kids:

Anne, Joe, Hank and Bill Skelsey, and Sue and Alice Huckaby.

Thanks also to a good green person who helped type the manuscript, Kathi Clement.

The kids growing up green in this book are
Jennifer, Suzanne, Christopher, Adam, Neil, Audrey, Peter, Alison, Betsey, Cathy and Garth.

and special thanks to Jennifer's father & Christopher's mother & father!

CONTENTS

PART ONE GROWING UP GREEN

1 *Discovering the Green World*

IT'S A STATE OF MIND

The surest way for a child to grow up green is to be exposed to parents who are still growing green. A child who has a preplanted terrarium purchased for him, who makes a once-in-grade-school field trip to an arboretum, who dines almost exclusively on processed foods isn't nearly so likely to grow up green as the child whose parents might stop to inquire what kind of plant the bank has growing in its lobby, to admire the beauty of an eggplant in the supermarket, to take home from a walk a leaf to identify, to share now and then a small tidbit of fact from nature, such as, say, when daffodils are blooming in the park—even when pressed a bit for time—you stop and take a deep, long look at them. After a few appreciative "Ooohs," small talk with a child might include counting the number of petals in the flower, followed by a did-you-know. A did-you-know, for example, that daffodils belong to a whole group of plants whose flower petals always come in sets of three?

Where the small talk meanders depends on the child's questions and your own knowledge of the subject. From Wordsworth via fourth grade comes to mind a few lines learned when such was required memory work:

> For oft, when on my couch I lie
> In vacant or in pensive mood
> They flash upon that inward eye
> Which is the bliss of solitude;
> And then my heart with pleasure fills
> And dances with the daffodils.

By junior high, it was Shakespeare, and a vagrant line surfaces:

> *Daffodils,*
> *That come before the swallow dares,*
> *and take*
> *The winds of March with beauty.*

You may feel, of course, that you don't know a great many green tidbits to pass along, but if you are in the process of growing green along with your child, you will be inquiring, observing, reading, learning as you go along, and what you learn you share as a matter of course when the occasion arises—easily, comfortably, companionably.

From the pleasure of watching a fern frond unfurl, you very much want to know about other plants of the same type. From your success with a turnip flowering and seeding in your windowsill, you move on to see what other second-generation vegetables might be produced there. From learning the names of the plants on the dime-store counter, you now find it almost impossible to pass a plant without wanting to know what its name is.

Actually the important thing that is passed along to your child is not the tidbit of information here or there, but the attitude —the awareness, the appreciation, the curiosity, the sharing, the love that makes growing up green inevitable.

Most important of all is to *be aware,* to *know* what is around you. Whether you are on a walk down a city street or through the woods, your child may very well be making more observations than you

named "catkins"

are. If you see little or nothing to pass on to him, if you
aren't observing and sharing with him, he may not keep that
sensitivity for long.

If, on the other hand, you can tell him the funny-sounding name of a
plant, or point out to him the pattern in the bark of a tree, how it differs
from another—one rough and cracked, and the other stretched smooth and
taut like the hide of an animal—or pick up a newly fallen seed pod to
inspect, you have made the event, no matter how small, something special.
A curiosity lodges, an interest begins, that if nourished will continue to
grow.

Part of the trouble, of course, is that adults can't share what they don't or no
longer have. After all, the major part of two older generations now have ties
remote from the land. For lots of grownups their own curiosity and knowledge of
nature got shut off at some point along the way without their quite knowing it.

As your own children grow, though, you can be led with them,
leisurely, from one interest to another in nature—a kind of tree, a type of
bird, a new planting for the terrarium. On occasion, with great enthusiasm, you
will be wanting to chase down new knowledge of the green world. You are never
too old to form ties to nature—and a most rewarding time to do it is while your
own children are growing up.

It is ironic in a day of deep and widespread concern for our environment that
books are even written on the importance of growing up green—and the necessity
for parents to help their children appreciate nature as a part of their everyday
lives. Whole institutions have arisen to deal with various crises, and along with
the inevitable bureaucracy they entail has come the inevitable depersonalizing of
the whole issue.

We can worry over the decline of the bald eagle, yet most of us will never see
one. We can wait anxiously for the current count on the whooping crane and we
can work up sympathy for the wolf as he is backed further and further into a
smaller and smaller part of his original territory. We may genuinely care about
these creatures, but ultimately they are abstract concerns.

Where environmental problems do touch us and our children personally, the emphasis is often on the ugly. Whole classrooms of children have been galvanized to fight pollution—an admirable cause—but not nearly enough time has been allotted to finding and appreciating the beautiful. A community youth group setting off to clean up a portion of a local stream or woodside focuses its attention on the beer can, not the beauty that still exists in the area. This is necessary, of course, for if one were to stop and admire the mosses, the wildflowers, the ferns along the way, far more beer cans would still be left scattered about at the end of the day. Still, combating the evils of technology's trash is not a substitute for positive encounters with nature.

Most of us *know* we are missing something. To feed our desire to renew our ties with the earth, to satisfy our yearnings for green and growing things, garden shops have sprung up as quickly and as widely as dandelions. Unfortunately, most of them have not the slightest relation to a child's interests or needs. Parents who seek greenery for their house or apartment may be content to install a four-foot potted plant in the corner of the living room. If that is the extent of their involvement in the green scene, they have invested about as much of themselves as parents who adopt a thirty-year-old, well- established businessman for a son. They have missed the life experience, the involvement, the point of the whole adventure—the chance to love, care for and watch over the development of a unique growing thing.

Parents, children and gardening ought to be perfect go-togethers. The basic ingredients of this triangle are fun and love, and when mixed together, you will find that all sorts of common interests take root, growing into ties between generations that can last a lifetime. Gardening is also the perfect antidote to a too-fast, too-complex world. It is like no other project, no other hobby. In fact, "project" and "hobby" do not define it well at all. Gardening is a way of life —a state of mind. It is not a set of steps to follow 1, 2, 3. What you hope your child will gain along with you is an enthusiastic, easy awareness that comes from day-to-day encounters with nature.

Even if you live in the heart of the city, gardening and nature can be much a part of your life. And the seemingly more remote you are from it, the more important to you that you seek it out.

Today, when so many of us long for a place in the country, a little bit of woods, or just a piece of farmland to which we can escape, we may make the mistake of postponing our enjoyment of nature until that dream comes true. The fact is, though, that most of us will not acquire that place in the country, and if we and our children are to grow up green on a daily basis we will have to take nature largely where we are.

There are many ways to bring it into our lives and into our children's wherever we live, even as we plan for a richer and simpler life later on.

On almost any shopping trip you make, a brief detour through the garden spot in the store will be rewarding. Today there is at least a small garden corner in almost every kind of store, dime, drug, department, discount. Maybe there won't be an extensive selection of plants in some of these places, but browse around through what there is. Many small potted plants today are marked with the names of the plants, where they come from, something about their ancestry and the kind of care they like.

You can make the acquaintance of almost all of the most commonly grown house plants with a minimum of time, no effort and lots of enjoyment. Share this experience with your children.

It is surprising and a bit sad how few children one sees in garden centers. And curious, too, that the proprietors seem not to have thought of children as customers. A children's garden corner could be a lovely place, with all kinds of plant displays high in appeal for the young—from spiny cactus to exotic orchids, from bonsai to banana trees. Birds from the pet department might await their adoption here. And there might be gardening supplies with special appeal to children— watering cans, little peat pots, bulb vases, nature books, flower holders— and artwork, originals of local artists as well as reproductions, from the beautiful and botanically exact mushrooms of Beatrix Potter to the unsurpassed still lifes of Cézanne.

When outdoors with your children—either for a special walk or simply on an errand—let them pick up leaves to take home. If you don't know which kinds of trees are which, help them look them up in an encyclopedia. Or borrow a book from the library and let the children play detective—searching for the pictures that match the leaves they have found. At the moment they match a leaf to a tree name, they will have formed a lasting curiosity about the trees they see. Send away for several garden catalogs, too.

And then there are special trips to make: to a big garden center or nursery, to an herb garden, to an arboretum or botanical garden. All of these places can open a wider world to all of us. Wherever you go, be sure to ask questions. What kind of plant is this? Will it grow in an apartment? How do you care for it? Gardeners— whether amateur, professional, business—are unfailingly generous in sharing with others the lore and love of plants.

Take snapshots of the children when they are planting, transplanting, harvesting, seed hunting or hanging the bird feeder. Such pictures can serve to pinpoint the events and give them the status of milestones in the children's lives—along with the first steps, the first day of school, the first this and that.

In the grocery store, teach them how to choose fresh vegetables. (They are parts of plants, you know, not just items that appear in the market from the back of a truck.) Never pass up a chance to stop, if only for a few moments, at a roadside or sidewalk vegetable or flower stand, to admire the goodies and chat with the proprietor, or even make a small purchase if you can manage it.

Another way to help make gardening a part of your life is to provide a specific place in your household for the supplies that go with it. That way, gardening can easily be translated into action when the opportunity presents itself.

The child who spots a curious-looking seed pod on the way home from school knows that gardening is a way of life at his house if he can take his treasure straight home to plant.

Planting seeds is no big deal to do, even if the child lives in an apartment. He simply takes a peat disk from a kitchen drawer, places it in a saucer of water, and waits a few minutes till it swells to become a tiny pot, with all the nourishment a seed needs to sprout and grow. Fun in itself for the child to do.

Having on hand the things you will need to garden—when the spirit hits you or the idea comes to your child—makes it much more likely that you *will* garden. It won't be necessary then to make a special trip to collect pots and planting medium, or to postpone with a promise, and more often than not, have that be the end of it.

Most successful projects for children, especially small children, require action and results. The quicker the better. But not so in gardening. There may be some action in the planting and the preparation—and then there is the waiting.

Your children will enjoy getting things ready for these sessions—preparing the pots, planting the seeds.

But then the action stops, and there may be long days when nothing much happens. Long days when nothing *at all* happens. The planted pot just sits where it is put.

Here it is better if you plan to carry the patience end of things yourself. Or mostly yourself. This means that you won't—please don't—hand over to your

child the waiting part of gardening as some sort of grim responsibility that will build character. "It's your garden; you're supposed to water it," is a wonderful way to turn children off from gardening. If you believe that your child will have learned a lesson should the garden fail, then spare him the lessons of gardening. All he will be doing years later is telling someone, "I just don't have a green thumb."

So don't involve your child in gardening with the idea that it will be "good" for him—that he will learn "responsibility" by tending his own plants. About as big a deal as you should make of a child's responsibilities to plants is to ask him if he has watered the plant—while you are on the way to water it yourself.

As the seeds come up, the plants grow, and flowers emerge and turn into fruit, then parents who have provided steady, supportive care to the plants can also share with their children the wonder of the miracle of life renewing itself from a seed, the beauty of its growth and the glory of its reproduction. Now, that is a lot! All of these things can be taught to kids by merely a "Look!" when a new happening has taken place in the flowerpot.

Seen from the child's point of view, there really are no disasters or failures in gardening: *whatever* happens will be interesting to him. The plant that dies can be dug up for a postmortem. Can he see that the soil is too wet, that the plant's stem has become heavy and waterlogged? The poor thing drowned. Or what about the plant that has become tall and spindly, its leaves yellow and sickly? It has been yearning for light, and without it, its root system has become thin and sparse.

You and your children will find enormous rewards in just a pot or two of a growing anything. Literally, anything. And from strictly gardening ventures your interests will branch out—as has this book—to embrace a love of nature, the study of birds, the preparation of good food, an appreciation of herbs. All this becomes part of the package as you grow with your gardening.

And consider what all this will give your children: a rapport with nature in all its diversity; a never-ending sense of wonder at the precision and beauty of it all; and a lifelong interest in growing things. Not bad dividends gained from an open heart.

So, remember, please, don't plan to "teach" your child with this little book. Gardening is caught—not taught. Enjoy!

19

START WITH A BEAUTIFUL DAY

An occasion that can imprint forever a joy in green and growing things is the celebration of a Beautiful Day.

A Beautiful Day is one you can actually feel physically. The moment you step out, you feel ten pounds lighter, even though you may have given up on your diet two months ago. The air *seems* clean and pure (no matter what the pollen or pollution count is telling you). The sky is blue. The clouds are of a particular puffiness or stretched sheerness, hung high in the sky and spaced with the greatest artistry.

Such days do happen in the city and are all the more to be watched for and treasured because they are the more infrequent there. Why should they go to waste? Why should they be enjoyed to the fullest only if by chance they land on a weekend? Why be bound to weather reports that tell us only of discomfort indexes and chill factors and never devote any official thought to guides to Beautiful Days?

Setting a definition for what makes a Beautiful Day is, of course, a highly individual undertaking for each family. Nonetheless, a number of the requirements can be quite specific. For example, determining the combination of measurable weather factors (temperature, humidity, wind velocity) can eliminate an inordinate amount of debate over whether the day does or does not qualify as a Beautiful Day.

In helping to decide what the combinations will be, your child will be observing each day much more carefully, comparing temperature and humidity combinations, peering at the sky, watching the wind—until the magic day comes up. He will become personally involved in and much more perceptive about the most pervasive part of nature—the weather. An outdoor thermometer placed where he can check it each morning is inexpensive and instructive for even the smallest child.

The combination or range of combinations of temperature, humidity and wind velocity are, of course, adjusted for each season. A Beautiful Day Index during spring, for example, might allow for a relatively high wind velocity if kite-flying enthusiasm is running strong in your family that particular spring.

What has flying kites to do with growing green? There is the whole point. If you must ask, you yourself have some growing yet to do.

You'll make your own kite, or course. Use a piece of gift wrapping paper—the brightest, gayest you can find. Let your child choose. Or use plain paper and let

Make a Kite!

36"

7"

29"

30"

22

him color his own kite design—a big, menacing face or a huge, bright flower.

A two-stick kite is easiest to make. You can get lightweight sticks of balsa wood at any hobby shop; or a piece of bamboo, split and quartered, will do. The measurements depend on the size you want. Just make the cross stick shorter than the long stick and place it a quarter of the way down the long stick.

Cut notches in both ends of both sticks. Put the sticks in cross position and tie them together securely at the point where the sticks cross. Now run a string around the kite through each notch, winding it around each notch several times as you go along to make the joints strong.

Now put the frame on the paper (paper upside down) and cut around it wide enough to leave a border of 2 inches all around. Paste this border over the string.

To make a harness (or bridle) for the string, turn the kite over, right side up. Tie a string about 4 inches longer than the cross stick, from one end of the cross stick to the other. Tie a second string about 4 inches longer than the upright stick, from one end of the upright stick to the other. At the center where the two strings meet over the cross sticks, attach your reel of flying string.

Now for the tail. Take another piece of string 4 or 5 feet long—the length can be adjusted after test flying. Tie small pieces of paper to the string (tissue paper is good) every 8 inches or so. Attach to the bottom end of the kite—and wait.

You're all set for a Beautiful Day of kite flying.

It takes a moderate wind to give a kite a good flight. Would you be able to look out your window and know from the leaves on the trees or in the streets whether a moderate wind was blowing—a wind of 13 to 18 miles an hour?

Of all of nature's elements, wind is the most elusive. Yet it can be one of the most instructive to observe. Noticing the specific effects of wind can teach perception in ways we don't ordinarily think about and sharpens our powers of observation.

Nearly 170 years ago an English admiral named Sir Francis Beaufort described the effects of various forces of wind, assigned them numbers, and put them in chart form.

BEAUFORT WIND SCALE

Beaufort No.	Description	Miles Per Hour	U.S. Weather Term
0	*Calm; smoke rises straight up.*	Less than 1	*Light*
1	*Smoke drifts.*	1-3	*Light*
2	*Leaves rustle.* *Can feel wind on face.*	4-7	*Light*
3	*Leaves and twigs move.* *Flags wave slightly.*	8-12	*Gentle*
4	*Raises dust and loose pieces of paper.* *Small branches move.*	13-18	*Moderate*
5	*Small trees sway.*	19-24	*Fresh*
6	*Large branches move.* *Hard to use umbrellas.*	25-31	*Strong*
7	*Whole trees sway.* *Difficult to walk against wind.*	32-38	*Strong*
8	*Twigs break off trees.*	39-46	*Gale*
9	*Larger branches break off trees.* *Some damage to roofs.*	47-54	*Gale*
10	*Trees uprooted.* *Not often experienced inland.*	55-63	*Storm*
11	*Widespread damage.*	64-73	*Storm*
12	*Devastation.* *Rarely experienced.*	74-more	*Hurricane*

With only a little experience in using the chart, you will be surprised at how rapidly you can become an expert on wind velocity. When you get up in the morning, you'll find yourself looking out the window first thing to check the leaves and branches of the trees for movement to help you estimate the wind speed. You'll look to see if stray papers are skidding on the pavement. Then you can call the telephone weather report to see how close you have come.

And, of course, each time you check the weather forecast for wind speed, you'll also be watching out for a possible upcoming B.D. combination.

Once you decide upon the factors that qualify for a Beautiful Day in your family, then comes the difficult part of deciding what to do about it when one arrives. The very brave—and the very lucky—may be able to pry loose a day of leave from work and school. Or maybe a few hours off early. Just once in the whole year, even! If it is a weekend, other pursuits could perhaps be abandoned or postponed a bit in place of enjoying the day itself.(Obviously, you have to be up reasonably early if you are to put the B.D. into effect. So any sleep-in days, while they may be good days, cannot also be Beautiful Days.)

Employers may not demonstrate a whole lot of enthusiasm for this custom, but exposure to the idea might be a good thing for all of us. A Beautiful Day needn't take away from the importance of school performance either. In fact, Beautiful Days can be great motivators. The uncertainty of when a Beautiful Day will appear can actually help youngsters prepare to make the most of the opportunity when it does arrive. School reports and projects and lessons somehow seem to be ready *before* they are due—just in case a Beautiful Day turns up. Which is only the other face of the same coin: where one generation might have been brought up learning the value of putting by for a *rainy* day, perhaps a new generation will do at least as well being prepared to seize the *sunny* one.

Ground rules for various activities may be necessary, too, to keep the Beautiful Day in line with the spirit. They should be largely devoted to enjoying the physical attributes of the Day itself and the rest of nature that shares it with us. (It is not a day when Dad takes off to play golf. Sorry, no. He can establish his own personal Golf Day Index, while Beautiful Days are kept separate—at least until the children are old enough so that Golf Days or such can be combined with Beautiful Days.)

Also, for Beautiful Days to be truly beautiful, they must be openly acknowledged for what they are. Which means that when you call the school, you don't say, "Sue isn't feeling well this morning, so I am keeping her home."

If you are being beautiful about it, you say, "I am keeping Sue home from school because it is a Beautiful Day." At the office you say, "Chief, boss, sir: I'd like to leave at noon if I may—it's a Beautiful Day at our house." Brave? Right!

What do you and your children do with your Beautiful Day? Well, if you have a spot of grass to stretch out on, and if the ground is dry enough by midmorning, for example, you can put an ear flat against it and listen. An enormous amount of activity is going on down under the earth—and children will love to listen in on it and guess what all the commotion might be.

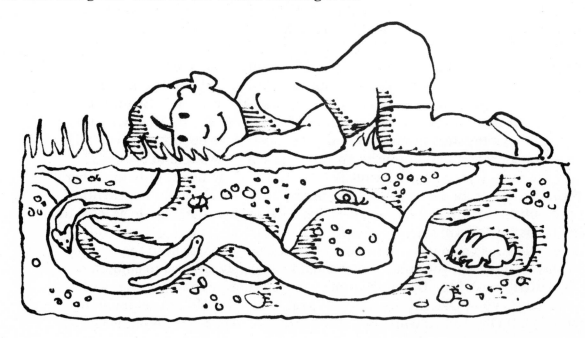

If it is spring, you can find a good spot to relax on and look up at trees and see patterns—one way or the reverse, trees against sky or sky against trees, as in optical illusions. Reversing views is an excellent lesson in perception and an ability many adults lose way back along the way in growing up.

If it is fall, you can pick out a single bare branch on a tree and trace every pattern it makes down to its tiniest twig.

Of course, absolutely smashing experiences may occur without planning. If it is nest-building time for squirrels, it might be your fortune that day to be stretched out and able to watch the scene for hours. You and your child can soon discover a pattern to their building. The particular tree they select, the particular branch they snip dry leaves from. Now, why does one squirrel run halfway across the park to take dry leaves from a tree when the tree with the nest has leaves right at its door? Is this squirrel just peculiar, or is there some reason for it? Do all squirrels follow this pattern in nest building? You resolve to ask the next squirrel watcher you bump into or to find out on your next trip to the library.

Or maybe you will decide to look for every sign of nature you can find in a two-block square stretch of crowded city sidewalks. Grass coming up through a crack in the sidewalk. Who would have thought? A few elm seeds scattered in a gutter. But where is the tree?—ah, yes, there is the top of it, showing down the street a block away. A fossil print in the stone on the side of a building—you're certain of it. A caterpillar crawling along the edge of the curb—where in the world could he have come from?

Or this is the day you will collect plants for pressings, or make a trip to an herb garden, or look for a spider web.

Another thing to do: look through the newspaper's classified ads for farms or country property for sale. Select one that sounds interesting and is easy to get to. Call and see if you can look at it. (Try for one that is owner-occupied so you won't have to involve an agent with your Beautiful Day, and thereby possibly ruin his or her day.)

During the preparation of this book, residents of the Washington, D.C., area woke up one morning in late February to bright sunshine, cloudless skies, a 7A.M. temperature near 40 degrees, humidity 59, wind velocity 5 miles per hour, a delicious scent to the air, and the unmistakable promise of a Beautiful Day in the making. All of this after days of sullen grayness, rain, snow watches and travelers' warnings.

At least one Beautiful Day Committee convened that morning, and . . .

TAKE A WOODLAND WALK

The suggestion of a woodland walk may have you thinking of a quiet patch of woods, sunlight dappling through the branches, a lifting spring day or a bracing autumn one. But a woodland walk can also be a stroll through a city park or even a walk through the apartment grounds—with the specific intent of looking for and at

the
trees—
the noblest,
grandest
green plants
of all.
Most people
don't usually think
of trees when they
think of gardening,
but trees are becoming
increasingly important to
all of us—especially to city
dwellers. We must have
these large green plants to
help purify our air, and
fortunately special thought
is now being given to
providing space and care
for all kinds of trees
—within shopping centers, in
parking lots, along curbsides.
So on your woodland walks
even in city areas, don't pass
the trees by without enjoying
them as part of nature.

A good game to play that can enhance your perception of the green world involves nothing more than setting a time limit for your walk—say, three minutes or five—during which each person concentrates on opening his senses to all the sights and sounds and smells of nature around him.

Then let the walkers make a list (not necessarily to be written down) of all the things their senses told them about nature. They saw the trees or the flowers or the grass, but did they really *see* them. Did they see the grass between the bricks or cracks in the sidewalks? Did they see the fungus growing on the side of an old tree in the curbside planting? Did they see that the roots of the tree are buckling the sidewalk from underneath? Did they *hear* the leaves rustling in the trees; did they *feel* the sun on their arms and faces; could they *smell* the green of the grass?

Any nature walk from then on will be full of many more perceptions. On special-occasion walks, plan to take along pencil and notebook, field glasses if you have them, a thermos of something cold to drink on hot summer days and the reverse in winter.

Look up for nests of tree animals. Squirrels build homes up in the highest branches of the tallest trees—there where you spot a large pile of leaves that seem to have been caught by the tree as they whirled by. In this raggedy tangle of leaves and twigs is a soft mattress of grass and feathers for the baby squirrels that will inhabit the nest in early spring.

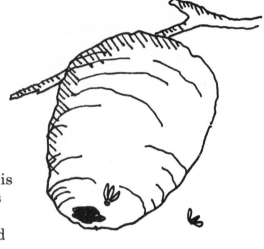

Should you spot a large round gray ball high up in the tree—that's the paper hornet's home. The paper from which its nest is made is homemade—by the hornet itself. The hornets chew up wood pulp, add their own juices to it, and mouthful by mouthful they spit it out and pat it into shape with their feet and mouths.

Take a special look, too, at the architecture of trees. The most familiar tree shape to children is the Christmas tree of the white pine, spruce, fir, or hemlock. But there is the Eastern cottonwood with its pear shape, bottom end up, and there is the sugar maple with its pear shape, bottom end down.

The chestnut tree may have its spreading branches, under which village smithies used to stand, but they are nothing compared with the spread of the live oak. And the willow oak discloses a great branchy Christmas-tree shape when it is bare of leaves.

Take a look at the various colorings of the trees. In winter the white trunks and limbs of the sycamores and birches stand out from the darker trees. Notice that the oaks hold onto their leaves to the very last, apparently waiting until all the other leaves have been neatly raked and composted before deciding to let go of theirs.

Look down, too, when you are nature-walking to see all the tiny, hidden things. A fiddleleaf just poking up; ground pine, green and healthy, winding its way under a covering of fallen leaves; a sudden small patch of cushiony moss; a tiny gem of a wildflower against the base of an enormous tree. Look carefully.

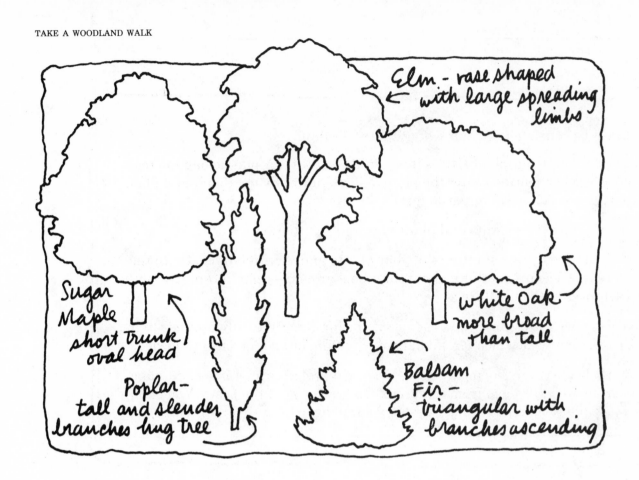

Look *carefully* at it all. Not one leaf exactly like any other on the same tree. Now, that is simply incredible. How precise the design, yet how unique each part!

Just because you don't know the names of what you are looking at, you shouldn't be discouraged from looking. You don't need to know *what* the plants are to enjoy their beauty or wonder at their oddity. Later—from a book, from a friend, or in a store or elsewhere—you will have the thrill of discovery that comes when you are able to match the name with a plant you know by sight.

LEARN ABOUT TREES

And why not adopt a tree of your own? No matter *where* you live, the decision
to adopt a tree can be a momentous occasion. Give the choosing of it a good deal
of thought before making a final selection. Consider those in your own yard,
on the apartment grounds, along the curbside or in the park.

After selecting your tree, you will then want to find out as much as you can about it. A special scrapbook will be fun to keep. Children love the idea of being photographed with their tree at different seasons of the year. The tree one sees in spring will not be the same tree in fall.

You can collect material from the tree—the new leaves of spring, the flower, the seed pod, fall leaves (or if you have chosen an evergreen, the cones and needles).

You can make a bark rubbing of your tree. Press a sturdy piece of paper—butcher's paper is good for this—against the bark. Rub with a piece of wax—kitchen paraffin or a piece of old candle with the outer layer scraped off will do. Charcoal will work, too, on a softer piece of paper, if you are careful to rub gently, with the charcoal laid flat so as not to break it.

You can also plant seeds from your tree and try your hand at bonsai-ing a whole, small grove of trees indoors.

Having learned a great deal about your own tree, you will then want to find out the names of your tree's neighbors. When you are into tree identification, you will notice many more things about the tree besides just the fact that it is a big green plant.

The shape of the leaves, for example. Some have "teeth" edges and others are plain. Some have a short leaf stalk, others long. Some have a rough surface, others smooth.

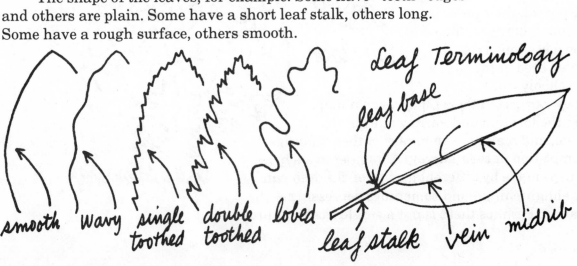

smooth wavy single toothed double toothed lobed

Leaf Terminology
leaf base
leaf stalk vein midrib

35

Then there are the seeds. Some, like the oak's, may come in cups; or in round balls, like the sycamore's; or in pods, like the locust's. Others may have wings, like the seed cases of the maple; or appear as berries, like those of the dogwood; they may be tiny like the elm's or huge like the coconut's. Some are found in fruit, like the Osage orange.

And all of this can lead to a tree census.

Children today are learning a great deal about our country's dwindling reserves of natural resources, and they are genuinely concerned about preserving our natural environment. One suggestion they will almost immediately act upon is a tree census. The census could cover their own yard, their immediate neighborhood, the downtown section, a certain designated area of the city, a park, a schoolyard.

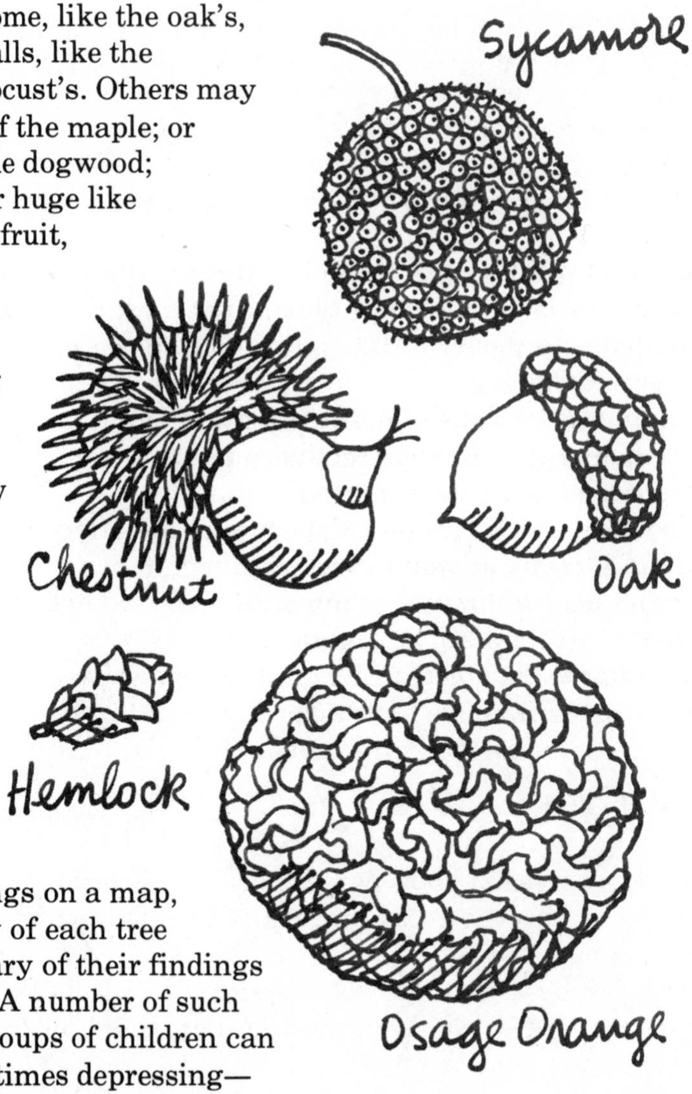

They can record their findings on a map, marking the location and variety of each tree as they go, and making a summary of their findings upon completion of their survey. A number of such census trips made by different groups of children can provide enlightening—and sometimes depressing—information. Perhaps there is not a single tree in or around

Sycamore

Chestnut

Oak

Hemlock

Osage Orange

36

a schoolyard. Why not a letter to the school board, asking if
you can plant some? You can grow your own. (See Seeds Along
the Way, page 155.)

The Great Tree Hunt

Where and what kind is the oldest tree in your community? The biggest tree?
The most historic tree? Such questions thrown out to a group of youngsters can be
quite a challenge to them. In their quest for answers, they will learn about history,
trees and the community.

Their findings will be of more interest to
the entire community than you might imagine.
If these trees have not received attention and
care, the youngsters can present their findings
to city officials (many communities are now
adding arborists or foresters to their staffs),
either in person or in a report, and request their
support for appropriate recognition and
attention for the trees.

Labeling Trees

If you have trees in your own yard, you are very lucky. But if you have been
passing them by, day after day, not really knowing much about them, then now is
the time to get acquainted.

The first order of business, of course, is to find out their names. And what
about the other plants in your yard—the shrubs and bushes that are planted close
around your house or apartment?

Find out all of their names. When you have identified them all, why not label
them so that your friends will know what they are when they meet them?

37

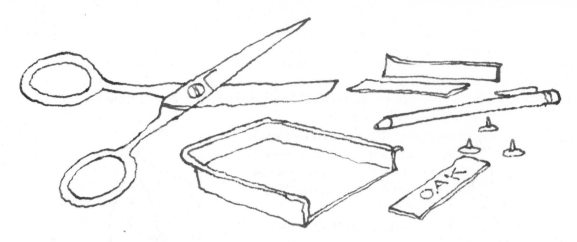

For labels, use the thin aluminum pans that frozen foods come in. These can be easily cut with a pair of scissors. (An old pair, please, not the ones that are used for sewing!)

Cut strips of the thin metal about 1 inch wide and 4 or 5 inches long. Now, with a ballpoint (with the pen part still retracted so you have a blunt end—not a sharp one that would puncture the metal) print the name of the tree carefully on the metal. You can make an indentation that will show up just fine and will last through all kinds of outdoor weather.

Since the metal is so thin, you will be able to fasten it to your tree with a couple of thumbtacks—which is much better for the tree than sinking nails into it.

All the plantings on your property can be name-tagged, giving them a bit of status and helping your friends learn to know them, too. For shrubs and bushes, punch a hold in one end of the metal tag and tie the name tag loosely around one of the branches.

You may want to use not only the common name of the plant but also its Latin name—for instance, pin oak, *Quercus palustris*. (See Following Famous Scientists, Carolus Linnaeus, page 91.)

If you own or have access to an etching needle, now widely used for placing identifying markings on personal property of all kinds, you have an ideal marker for making tree labels of metal. With such a good marking tool at hand, you can, with a little practice, print or write out your labels in a neat, professional manner.

Tree Cards

Here is a set of cards you can make yourself and have a new card game to play with friends—children and adults both.

Collect the leaves of as many different trees as you can. Carefully trace the outline of each leaf on a piece of cardboard. (Manila file folders are stiff enough; boards from the laundry and poster paper will work, too. The stiffer the better, though.)

Cut out along the lines to make a card silhouette of each leaf. For an attractive set of cards, draw in the veins and color the leaf drawings on one side. On the back side print the names of the trees.(Aha, here is some identification work for you to do if you don't know the names, right?)

You can play tree cards by dealing the cards out, leaf side up in front of each player. Take turns identifying the leaves, one leaf to a round. If a person cannot identify a leaf, he must pass. If he can identify the leaf, he puts it in his "stack." When a player cannot identify a leaf in his hand and must pass, the next time around he may, on his turn, identify—and claim—a leaf in another person's hand. The player with the largest number of leaves in his stack at the end of the game wins.

It won't be long before you and your friends will know all the leaves by heart. Then to make things a little tougher, sit in a circle on the floor and deal the cards behind the back of each person. Now, the players must reach behind their backs, and by using their fingers only (and no peeking), they must try to identify the leaves by touch—feeling the shape of each leaf to tell which is which.

If a player cannot identify the first leaf he picks up, he must pass. If he chooses, he can also pass the leaf on to the person on his left, then draw a new leaf from the person on his right, and await his next turn to try for another identification.

Water Witching

Just for fun on woodland walks, keep your eye out for a small tree branch that has a fork in it—a branch shaped something like a wishbone. With this branch, you can try your hand at water witching!

Hold on to two ends of the forked branch with the palms of your hands facing up. Walk slowly holding the branch so that it points straight up. When you approach a source of moving water, even through an underground water pipe, you, will feel a pull on the branch as it begins to move toward the earth. When you are directly over the water (and *if* you have the powers of a water witch!), the branch will be pointing straight down even though you try your best to hold it up.

Water witching works for some people and not for others. Those it doesn't work for are usually inclined to think the whole thing is a fairy tale. Those it does work for believe that water witching (also called "dowsing") is a power only some people have. Either way, water witches throughout history, and to the present day, have been called on to use their divining rods to help locate sources of underground water.

Water witches say that a forked stick from almost any sort of tree will work, but the preferred species seem to be peach, apple, willow and maple.

40

LEARN ABOUT BIRDS

      Since there is no way a person can grow up green without becoming a bird watcher, too, the sooner you start the better. A whole new hobby world will open to you—one that is easy, fun and free.

      Once you decide to take a good look at the birds, you will be charmed by the differences among them—not only in their markings but in their habits and personalities. The fussy, busybody wren; the placid, minds-its-own-business mourning dove.

A child doesn't need binoculars to enjoy bird watching. In fact, for small children, a pair of binoculars can become a distraction. They will enjoy making field glasses out of their hands. Show them how to cup their fingers around their eyes to eliminate side distractions. Keep thumb and forefinger apart where they meet at the nose. The forefinger lies along the eyebrow, the thumb is below the eye and the rest of the fingers are curved in front of the forefinger, shading the eye.

For the older bird watcher, a good pair of field glasses can add greatly to the pleasure of this pastime. Choose a pair of glasses that have a wide field of vision. A narrow field of vision (such as one has with a telescope) requires accuracy in finding and focusing on a particular distant spot. The child must turn this way and that to find the spot, and meanwhile the bird may have departed. So glasses with a wide field of vision are a must for the growing bird watcher.

The next step up from bird-watching is a bird book of your own. Here you can begin a record of all the different kinds of birds you see, with dates and places, too. Confirmed birders call these "life lists."

If you remember to look for different types of birds while on vacations and other trips, you can log dozens of different birds in your book. (You'll see lots of birds, for example, on a slow drive down a country road.) Birding can be an incidental but enormously fun part of seeing different places.

For the first year of birding, you might set a goal of sighting twenty different species of birds around your home. That would be a good number for the suburban child to attain, and an even greater coup for the city child.

While new bird sightings may be more infrequent after the first couple of years, by that time the excitement has become all the greater when you do spot a new addition for your book. In between new finds, you can keep count of the number of different birds seen at your feeders at any one time, or for the season; the date of first appearance of summer and winter birds; and data on migrating birds. The latter can be especially exciting when a whole flock of birds, such as the evening grosbeak, drop in to spend a few hours or a few days at your feeder.

Your book will be especially interesting if you plan to include more than just a listing of birds sighted. You can, for example, include a page for your own drawing of each kind of bird you see. You can also attach bird feathers you find to the appropriate pages.

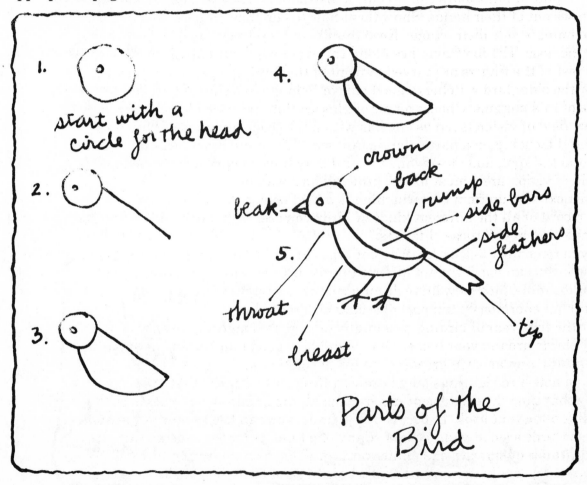

1. start with a circle for the head

2.

3.

4.

5. beak- crown back rump side bars side feathers throat breast tip

Parts of the Bird

For your book choose a soft-cover, loose-leaf binder. If smaller than the normal school size, it will be easier to tote along on trips. Plan to allow two facing pages for each bird. On the left-hand page you will want to leave a place for listing the bird's name; the date you sighted it; the date you identified it (not always the same as when first seen!); where; time of day it feeds; activities that distinguish it from other types of birds; and other observations of your own.

On the opposite page you can include your own drawing of the bird. If you don't consider yourself much of an artist, here is a simple method of drawing birds that will also help you fill in different identifying marks.

By concentrating on only a few main parts of the bird, you can quickly learn most of the important identifying color marks. Checking for such markings makes coloring your own bird drawings much more fun. Use pencil colors—they are easier to work with than crayons for this type of color work.

For the head: Check these three main parts—the beak, the crown and the throat. Eye stripes and eye rings can come later.

For the body: The breast, the back and the rump.

For the wings: Look for side bars and flash marks (seen when the bird flies).

For the tail: Side feathers and tips (when resting) and flash marks (when in flight).

There are still other things a child can look for in identifying birds besides color and markings.

Birds have different kinds of feet. The feet of the woodpecker and nuthatch and wren tell a great deal about how these birds live.

Feet

Woodpecker (holding)

Osprey

Duck (swimming)

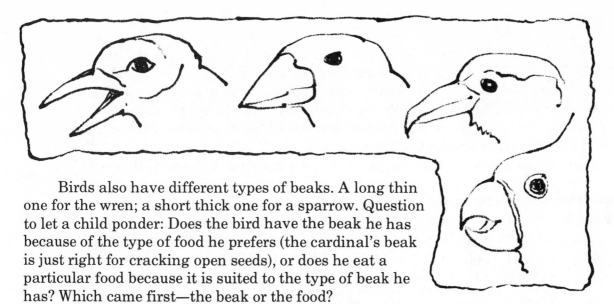

Birds also have different types of beaks. A long thin one for the wren; a short thick one for a sparrow. Question to let a child ponder: Does the bird have the beak he has because of the type of food he prefers (the cardinal's beak is just right for cracking open seeds), or does he eat a particular food because it is suited to the type of beak he has? Which came first—the beak or the food?

How the bird holds its tail is another identifying trait. You could never mistake a little brown wren for a little brown sparrow, if only by the way they hold their tails. The wren cocks its tail over its back; the sparrow's tail droops down.

Some birds feed on the ground; others will not. Some others hop. A robin fairly bounces along. A starling walks . . . well, actually, it lurches. A blackbird strolls, a mourning dove waddles—slightly.

The song of the birds is another lovely part of the green world awaiting your discovery. Some bird experts will tell you that birds sing to communicate with each other: to warn of danger, to tell of food, to attract mates.

Bird lovers are also certain that some birds sing simply because they like to sing. Watch a mockingbird running through his repertoire and you will have no doubts—he sings because he does it well, and he enjoys it!

Many public libraries have records of bird songs available for loan. These can provide a great deal of listening pleasure for children and grownups alike, especially if followed up with an outing to scout for those same songs performed by the original cast. Children, particularly, find it enormously satisfying to be able to recognize a feathered friend nearby without even having seen it.

> *That's the wise thrush; he sings each song twice over,*
> *Lest you should think he never could recapture*
> *The first fine careless rapture!*
>
> —Robert Browning

Obviously, bird-watching and bird-feeding are go-togethers and you will find that winter feeding provides the most in bird-watching on all counts. You will see more birds at this time of year because there is much less food available to them from other sources, and you will be able to see them better when the trees are bare.

Once you begin feeding the birds they will stop looking elsewhere for food. Should a snow come and cover any other obvious sources of food and you haven't put out your regular supplies, a lot of your birds will go hungry and possibly starve. So once you begin bird-feeding in the wintertime you must hold up your end of things and keep your feeders supplied until spring.

If you don't have trees or shrubs close to your house for birds to perch in, then after Christmas look for cast-out Christmas trees. Just one or two of these (but the more the better) propped up in a clump (and the more clumps the better) can entice more birds to your feeders. For one thing, the birds will be able to flit from the feeders to the security of the branches should a marauding cat appear on the scene. (After all, who could eat while the possibility exists that a monster might pounce on you at any moment.) The Christmas trees, even though cut, will stay green enough for the rest of the winter.

The best approach to bird-feeding is cafeteria-style, where different birds can choose the different sorts of food they like. And place the tables to suit their preferences, too: hang some feeders from branches; spread other feed on the ground, or close to it; attach suet, orange rinds and such to the trunks of trees.

Feeders and houses do not have to be elaborate to suit the birds, and the homemade kind always has more character. Plastic gallon milk containers make excellent feeders and are quick and easy for children to turn out. Here are several pointers:

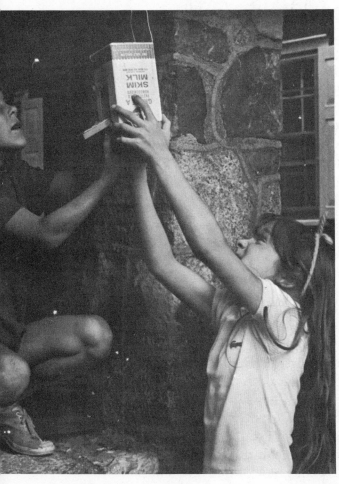

● Leave at least 2 inches at the bottom to hold the feed securely inside the feeder. In a strong wind, your feeder may swing back and forth, and with a too-shallow base most of your feed can wind up on the ground. A rock put in the feeder will also add weight and make it more stable.

● Punch a few holes in the bottom of the feeder so that any blown-in rain will drain out.

● For easy cutting of the plastic, fill the container with hot water, let stand for 5 or 10 minutes and pour out. Now you will find the plastic soft and easy to cut.

● Some birds like to perch close to their feed source, so punch a couple of holes in the sides of the container and run a stick through it with ends projecting on each side. Tie a string around the top or through the handle and hang. Be sure to leave the cap on so the rain won't run in through the top!

● Most birds seem to prefer woodsy, subdued nature colors (the hummingbird is an

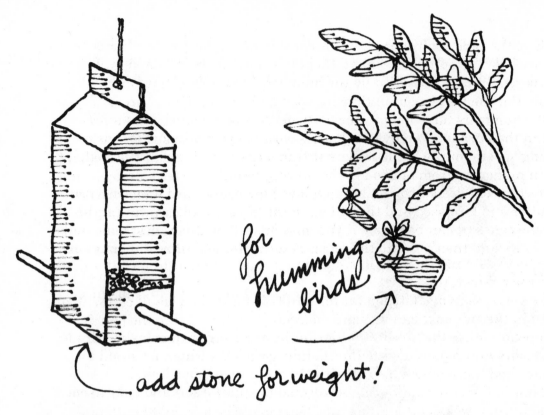

for hummingbirds

add stone for weight!

exception), so before cutting the container you might want to
spray-paint the outside a soft brown, green or grey.

Since one species or another of hummingbirds is common in nearly every
part of the United States, it is worth your while to try to attract these beautiful
and smallest of birds. They require almost constant feeding to keep themselves
going. If you watch their nonstop whirring wings (even while feeding) you'll
understand why.

For the special tastes of hummingbirds, combine ⅛ cup of sugar with ⅞ cup
of warm water. Stir till sugar is dissolved, and add red food coloring to make the
solution a good bright pink (hummers are attracted by the color). Pour into small

bottles (such as the type aspirin or vitamins come in or smaller), tie a red ribbon around the necks of the bottles and hang them to a bush or shrub—preferably a flowering type that might be visited by the hummers, but failing that, any nearby shrub. Put the feeders out in time for spring blooming in your area.

After the hummers have found your bottle-feeders and visited them a few times, you can then gradually move the bottles closer to your window for easier viewing. Hang several of the bottle-feeders within a few feet of each other so the hummers can maneuver from one to another during feeding.

Other feeders children enjoy making include pine cones filled with a mixture of peanut butter and bird seed and then hung in the trees. Or kitchen fat can be poured into the cones (it can be messy if you miss or spill, so this is best done over the kitchen sink), and then put into the refrigerator to harden before the cones are hung out in the trees. Prop them up in small paper cups or in muffin pans for their brief stay in the refrigerator.

Another way to salvage kitchen fat for bird-feeding is via a small can with a hole punched in the side so it can be hung on a nail on a tree. Using the punch type of can opener, make the hole in the side of the can near the top; it can then be taken down easily and replaced with a refill. Refrigerate the can of fat first to harden it, and then hang it outside on the tree.

Beginning birders are cautioned not to put out metal for bird baths, nests or most feeders. In cold, wet weather, the birds' feet may stick to a metal bath or feeder. However, a small can of fat that fits snugly to the side of a tree allows woodpeckers, nuthatches, and other tree-clinging birds to remain on the tree and sample the fat from the cans. Squirrels, too! Use small, shallow cans—the flat, tuna-size types.

A coconut sawed in half (even better, a quarter of it taken out) can be hung, with some of the coconut meat left in, as a special treat for the birds. Later, when the shell is empty, it can be used as a regular feeder. If you use the end with the "eyes" for the bottom of the feeder, they can serve as drain holes.

Leftover halves of oranges and grapefruit, after the insides have been squeezed or eaten, can also be impaled on a nail for birds to pick clean.

Every kitchen scrap you can spare for the birds should be saved. Bird seed, sunflower seeds, raisins and such can be expensive; and the more you have, the more successful you become at attracting customers. You will want to save all cantaloupe and other melon seeds; any leftover bits of fruit, even apple cores and such; leftover or stale bread and rolls.

Crumble the bread first before putting it out for the birds, else a squirrel may carry away the whole thing, or you will attract more starlings than you may want.

Squirrels present an extra added attraction when you take up bird-feeding. They are inventive acrobats and will outwit every sort of contraption you can rig up to keep them away from the feeders. Since they are such lively visitors, and since they have hunger pains, too, the trick is to provide for them and still keep them from wiping your feeder clean before the birds have had a chance to eat.

Feeding a good number of birds can be expensive if you must buy food (which is why you grow, save and collect as much as you can for them). But squirrels can eat you out of house and home! So in late summer and early fall especially, watch out for acorns, other tree nuts and all kinds of tree, weed and flower seeds that are scattered about, even on sidewalks and city streets, that might otherwise go to waste. Collect these and tie them in plastic bags to save for the squirrels when winter comes.

You will not find in these pages any foolproof method for keeping squirrels away from your bird feeders. Only a word of caution: Don't underestimate these wily, furry fellows. Their death-defying feats include hanging upside down by the toes of their back feet while stuffing their faces from a feeder you thought absolutely, totally beyond their reach; making flying leaps through the air to smack their bodies against a feeder with enough force to make it swing violently and dump its contents on the ground; or climbing to the topmost part of a tall tree, threading their way out to the very tip of the longest branch and in true Tarzan

fashion catapulting themselves on to the platform of a feeder that had been carefully protected by a squirrel baffle from below. Yes, it is great sport to pit your own wits against those of the squirrels. And may the smartest one win!

Birds need water, too, of course—not only for drinking but also for bathing. They love to bathe and put on a great show when splashing about in their tub.

The lid of a heavy-duty plastic trash can makes a good bird bath. Prop it up off the ground with a few bricks or rocks or branches or whatever. A metal bath will not do. Ceramic or pottery isn't satisfactory, either, for use in weather cold enough to freeze water, for as the water expands in freezing, the dish will crack.

Birds like to bathe near the ground—no higher than 3 feet or so, and many prefer their tub lower. They also like to bathe out in the open rather than close to low shrubbery or bushes where a cat might lie in waiting.

Also, plan to help the birds along at nest-building time in late winter and early spring. Simply save scraps of yarn, string, small strips of rags, thread, twine. Place these in a mesh bag and hang in a tree where the birds can come and choose what they need.

Or you can weave a special nest-maker for your birds. Pull a coat hanger into a rectangular shape. Slip a mesh bag (the kind potatoes or oranges come in) over the hanger. Weave your scraps of yarn and thread through it. Hang it in a tree, not too high up—no more than 6 feet. Now you will have fun watching the birds make their selection of building materials and pull them from the nest-maker. Later on in the spring, take a stroll through your neighborhood looking for birds' nests and see if you can spot pieces of the yarn you put out.

Lots of interesting, informative, and intriguing conversations between parent and child can arise during the most casual day-to-day bird-watching.

Bill: I wonder if there is such a thing as a bachelor bird?

Mother: You mean some birds might decide that family life is just not for them?

Bill: No. My bird books are always talking about birds choosing their mates. Is there always an equal number of males and females so no one gets left out? What does a bird do if it can't find a mate?

Mother: My gosh. I've never thought about that before. (Good grief! What do they do?)

52

2 The ABC's of Gardening—
Indoors & Out

GETTING STARTED

Getting Started Indoors

All gardeners, down to the very youngest, enjoy the getting-started part of gardening almost the best—deciding what to plant and preparing the seed bed (the latter an interesting term, since seeds are placed there not to put them to sleep but to wake them up).

The bed can be made from a large milk carton, turned on its side and the top side cut out of it; or aluminum foil loaf pans or 1-pound coffee cans. Whatever the child decides on, he should punch holes in the bottom of it so that excess water will be able to drain out of it.

As for the soil, premixed potting soil is available wherever gardening supplies are sold. It is well worth the small investment to get your seeds off to a good start. The soil mix has been sterilized and treated to reduce the dangers of plant disease or fungus that might be encountered in the use of ordinary dirt.

The children will first fill the containers they have chosen for the seed bed to within a half-inch of the top and smooth out the surface. Then they can water the bed with a fine spray until it is damp throughout. Or they can place the entire bed in a sink or other large container and let it soak up water from the bottom. When the surface of the bed appears damp, they will know that the soil mix is damp throughout.

Now it is planting time. Elbow the kids out of the way long enough to point out to them just how small the seeds are (if they are) and that the little envelope they are in must be tapped gently so that only a few seeds fall out at a time. They won't

plant the seeds as precisely as the seed packet instructs nor as carefully as you would, perhaps, but it will make less difference to the seed than you would suppose as long as they are reasonably close to the specified planting depth.

Once the seeds are placed on the surface of the damp bed, the children can press them gently but firmly into the soil with the palms of their hands. Then they can sprinkle more damp potting soil over the seeds to the planting depth specified on the seed packet.

Now the bed can be covered with a piece of clear plastic wrap and placed on a windowsill where it will receive light, but not direct sunlight. Within a few days, the first signs of new life will appear—maybe one or a half-dozen tiny greenish white loops. The stems and curled-under leaves emerging signal the beginning of a new life cycle. It is an exciting moment.

Remove the plastic wrap and gradually introduce the bed to more light over the next few days. The first two leaves to unfold from the safety of the seed covering are called the heart leaves. At this point, you can hand your child a small pair of scissors (manicure, sewing) and let him thin out all but the number of plants he wants to keep—or remove at least all those that are so close the leaves are touching each other. He can reach in and snip off close to the soil all the surplus seedlings.

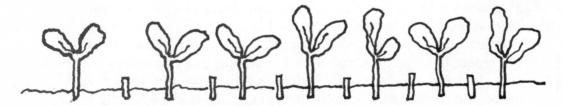

The heart leaves are soon followed by another pair of leaves, different-looking from the first. These are called true leaves—the leaves of the mature plant. When the second set of true leaves appear, the seedling is usually large enough to be transplanted to individual containers or outdoors if the weather is dependably warm.

55

Forcing apart the tangled roots of little seedlings and planting them individually in larger pots or outdoors may cause some "transplant shock" to the small plants, which could result in arrested growth or puny specimens. So it is important to help the children handle the seedlings with care during transplanting.

If you are dealing with a house plant which is to remain indoors, have the new container all ready—good drainage provision; soil soaked until moist throughout. The seedlings should also be thoroughly watered before transplanting. Carve each seedling away from its fellows with the handle of a teaspoon or other small digging tool, and lift it from the flat, trying to keep as much soil as possible about its roots. Set it in the permanent container and firm the soil about the roots and the stem. Place the new transplant on a north windowsill but not in direct sunlight for the next two or three days while the roots are taking hold in their new container. Gradually introduce the plant to more sunlight.

If you are dealing with seedlings that are destined for outdoor locations, transplanting should be preceded by a period of "hardening off." This simply means that the seedlings are introduced to outdoor conditions gradually. The first day, for instance, put the seedling bed outside in a place protected from the wind and not in direct sun, for about two or three hours in the morning. Gradually increase the plants' outdoor time and sunlight over the next week or ten days, bringing them back indoors on chilly nights. Be sure that the bed never dries out during this time. Then when transplanting to the garden, follow the same general procedure as for house plants. Have the ground damp but not muddy. And have the seedling flat damp. Prepare holes in the ground for the prospective transplant. Tomatoes and pepper plants can and should be set deeper in the ground than they were in the seedling bed. Set them as deep as the first pair of leaves. It will help give them protection against the wind and will also help them to develop a stronger root system. Firm the soil around the roots and stem, leaving a slight depression all around the stem of the planting so that water will be retained there.

You will have to be especially watchful now that the young plants are outdoors to see that their water needs are met and that they do not receive too much strong sun. If you notice the plants are wilting but the soil about them is damp, they are probably getting too much sun. Rig a temporary shade from cardboard cartons, newspapers or whatever until the plants have overcome the transplanting trauma and begin to grow anew.

In recent years new items have appeared on the garden scene that can eliminate many of the problems associated with transplanting. Of special appeal— and especially helpful—for the child gardener is the peat pellet. It is a flat disk about 2 inches in diameter and about ¼ inch thick, made of compressed soil, nutrients and peat. When put in water, it expands to about 2 inches in height in just a few minutes. This magic alone is enough to lure any child into the planting action.

You plant the seed right in the little soil-filled "pot." The whole thing is enclosed in a thin netting which holds the soil together and allows the plant's roots to grow through. The pellets save the cost and bother of using potting soil, eliminate the need for starting flats, are quick, easy, and clean; and when the young seedling is ready to go into its permanent growing quarters, you simply plant the peat pot and all. These gardening goodies cost from 5 to 10 cents each, depending on the number bought at one time. They are available in most garden supply stores or can be ordered from seed catalogs.

The planted peat pots can be placed in muffin tins, on a tray, or in cake pans for ease in handling numbers of them at a time. The tray can be slipped into a plastic bag which is then twisted closed. (Greenhouses are not the exclusive province of the professional gardener. If you have a plastic bag, you have a greenhouse.) As soon as the seeds begin to sprout, remove the plastic bag and place the pots in as much light as you can manage, but not direct sunlight. As with the seedlings sown in beds, the hardening-off procedures should be followed before transplanting outdoors.

Preplanted beds (flat) and preplanted peat pots are also newer garden aids. These doubtless take much of the "work" out of planting, but they also take much of the fun out of it for the children. You are also limited as to the varieties of seeds available.

Getting Started Outdoors

If seeds are to be sown directly outdoors, a whole new vista is opened to youngsters involving a rather grand activity known as Getting the Ground Ready. Ideally, getting the ground ready should start in late fall when the area to be planted the following spring is turned with a spade or pitchfork and left to freeze and thaw repeatedly all during the winter months. Many insects and weed seeds which normally winter over in the first few inches of topsoil are dispatched by following this procedure.

Even if getting the ground ready is not commenced until late winter or early spring, it is still an awe-filled experience. On a fine day in February or March the leaves are raked away from the garden plot, and if the ground is not too wet, the first shovel of earth is turned. The true rites of spring begin.

Let the youngsters participate as much as possible in the preparation of the garden spot. There will be a great deal more satisfaction to be gained from this land than just the crops that can be grown there. You will likely have much to do to your ground and to learn from it before you ever plant it.

First thing is to stake off the planting area to protect it from being trampled if it is in a high-risk area of walkers or bicyclists.

Next is to improve on the dirt itself. If, for example, the only garden space you have is close to the wall of your house or apartment, the chances are that the soil is something less than great for gardening. The backfill put in after construction is hardly ever (let's face it, *never*) composed of good topsoil. Here, then, is where you and the children can see firsthand the value of caring for and restoring the land. Replenishing depleted soil, altering the structure of heavy clay so that it will drain well or of sandy soil so that it will hold moisture better—these are things that can help your garden flourish and tie you directly to Mother Earth.

Also, here is where "organic" gardening can mean something specific to your child. For to get his patch of ground in shape, he will need to put back into the soil organic matter—things that were once living. Material that once came out of the earth is put back. Food scraps, potato peelings, eggshells, apple cores—all can be dug into the garden spot.

You must have a few garden tools on hand, and among them a small shovel comes first. Leave it close by the garden so that it will be handy for burying your kitchen treasure, otherwise known as garbage. For the small child, choose a hand trowel, but make it a good sturdy one. (Army surplus stores have great little folding shovels—designed for foxhole digging, but perfect for youngsters' gardening activities.) Show your child how to bury the kitchen leavings efficiently. As one batch of organic material is buried, a hole should be left to receive the next batch.

Fallen leaves can also be gathered, crumbled up, and dug into the ground. When you or the older children are handling the shovel, dig down at least 8 inches—a foot deep is even better. Plan on digging into the ground all of the organic material you can get your hands on, right through fall and winter up to planting time in the spring—whenever the ground is workable. Obviously it is not workable when frozen, nor should it be worked when wet and soggy because of damage to soil structure.

All of the organic material you bury in your garden will gradually be broken down and the soil will become loose and airy and crumbly (friable, the soil scientists call it).

If you have some doubts about the capability of your soil to produce honest-to-goodness vegetables, have a soil test made to determine any deficiencies it might have. Look in the phone book for the office of the county agent (listed under county or city government, under Cooperative Extension Service, or under State University). The county agent's office can tell you where to send your soil sample for free testing. There are also inexpensive soil-testing kits on the market which even a young child can use to determine the condition of the soil and what if any minerals should be added to it. Sometimes a bag or two of lime, potash or fertilizer is indicated, and it is much easier to work this material into the soil as the garden site is prepared rather than try to work it in after planting.

After several sessions with the land, you will yield to your own or the youngsters' demands to plant this and plant that. Onion slips are the first entry in almost every outdoor garden, usually in February, as they can withstand the freezing temperatures yet to come in March and April. But the planting of most other vegetables will have to wait until all danger of frost has passed. You won't be idle, of course, if you are starting your tomatoes, peppers and other plants indoors. Seed packet instructions will help you on timing your outdoor plantings for the area in which you live.

The arrangement of plants to make in the outdoor garden is more a matter of preference than prescription. (Check the ideas in Mini-Farming, pages 109-126.) Whatever planting arrangement you and your child decide on, be sure to leave enough space between rows so that plants can be reached for weeding and watering.

Very small seeds, such as carrot and radish seed, can be difficult for children to handle in outdoor planting. Mix them with very fine soil and then they can pour the soil along a planting furrow they have made in the ground.

Seed tapes (seed impregnated in a water-soluble organic tape) can be fun for children to try. They are easy for little fingers to handle, eliminate the need for thinning plants out later on and also eliminate waste and guesswork in spacing the seeds. For the purist, tapes may take out a little of the "feel" of gardening but they can put in a lot of fun. They can be curved and shaped into designs during the planting process or make the perfectly straight rows that a young perfectionist might crave. The Geo. W. Park Seed Company, has possibly the largest offering of seed tapes—over a hundred flower varieties, thirty-four vegetables and five herbs. You can order them or possibly find them in discount houses, variety stores and some grocery stores on the seed racks along with conventionally packaged seeds.

FOLLOWING THROUGH

Following Through Indoors

Children can't go far wrong in caring for their plants if they start with these general rules.

Water: Don't overdo. Check your plants daily. If the surface of the soil feels dry and crumbly, add water. Don't water again until the soil feels dry. Empty any water that remains in the saucer after an hour's soaking.

Food: During blooming and fruiting times, a three-week interval is a good average for feeding. All-purpose plant food is available in powder or liquid form. Be sure to dilute to proper concentration before applying. Read the label carefully.

Light: Plants will signal when not getting enough light: turning a pale green color and waving their leaves from spindly stems. Flowering plants need sunlight and will do better in south windows, while foliage plants will receive the light they need, but not direct sun which they don't need, in a north window.

Remember these four requirements for preparing a good container-home for your plant:

1. Hole in the bottom for drainage.
2. Pebble, screening, shard—something loose-fitting over the hole to let water run out but keep soil in.
3. A layer of gravel—more good drainage insurance against wet feet for plants.
4. Potting soil, with nutrients added regularly when the plant is making growth.

Remember these Don'ts:

1. Don't put plants near radiators or other heat sources.
2. Don't keep them on *drafty* windowsills.
3. Don't change their environment abruptly.

And these Do's:

1. Do be consistent in your watering and feeding.

2. Do arrange for plant sitters if you must be away. A plastic bag makes a good weekend sitter. Water the plant, as you normally do, then put a plastic bag over it. This will make do for a few days.

3. Do share your plants and plant know-how with others.

4. Do make the acquaintance of your plants and their relatives. Go to the trouble to learn something about their background—their botanical family, their origin, their culture.

5. Do visit with your plants each day. During this time, tidy up their living space, remove dead leaves, give them a dusting or sponge bath if needed.

6. Do be alert for "enemy attacks." You will probably spot insect damage (leaf holes, sticky goo from scale, etc.) before you spot the pests. You can rid house plants of a good many pests by simply washing them off with a fine spray mist.

Following Through Outdoors

As your plants mature in the garden, you will find yourself dealing mainly with two problems: keeping down weeds and keeping up moisture. For both these problems, mulch can help. Actually no gardener is a gardener unless he is, or has been, involved with mulch. The sound of the word exactly matches what mulch looks like and what it does: loose, crumbly stuff—from leaves, grass clippings, seed

hulls, husks and other chopped-up, shredded plant material—that you spread on the ground, usually around plants, as a snuggly, protective blanket. A mulch keeps the soil from drying out too fast on hot days, keeps weeds from popping up where they aren't wanted, and keeps the soil from running away with the rain.

Those who know nothing about mulches (as well as those who know too much about mulches) believe that homemade mulch involves a backbreaking, long-term, complicated process, completely out of reach of the ordinary green person, not to mention those with limited access to shovels, shredders and all the rest.

Well, there is not all that much mystique to mulch, and certainly children ought to get acquainted with its making as early on as possible.

You will need only a large plastic trash bag; dead leaves; some dirt—not a whole lot; lime, bought by the bag in a hardware or garden shop; and water.

Fill the bag about one-fourth full of leaves; toss in a light layer of dirt (known as soil to some people), a cup of lime, and a cup of water, unless the leaves are already partly wet, in which case cut down on the water.

Repeat till the bag is full, then tie it up with a twistum and that's it.

You will have started your sack of mulch in the fall with the fallen leaves, and so you stack it aside until spring. In between times, you might want to give the bag a turn upside down every once in a while—two or three times, say, between fall and spring—and on each occasion open the bag to let new air in, too.

In the spring you will have nice—that is to say, mulchy—mulch. The bacteria in the soil, the lime, the water, have all worked on the leaves to break them down into a crumbly, soft material—delicious for plants. Spread it under the plants in your yard or around the newly planted crops in your five-foot farms.

Food crops, especially, must have water and lots of it. When rain does not supply a good soaking every few days or more often in really hot weather, then be ready with some kind of bucket brigade if you do not have access to a garden hose. Needless to say, children will enjoy either effort here. In fact, you may have to keep repeating to yourself that all of this is "fun" as the water lands lots of places other than on the plants. After a while, though, the water play eases off and the garden gets more water in less time. And, anyway, it's good to keep in mind that a successful outdoor farm for parents and children mixes play with work in such a way that no one can tell for sure which is which.

In any event, make certain the plants get a good soaking. A twice-a-week thorough watering is much better than a light watering every day. For children to remember to give each of their plants a good big deep drink of water whenever it needs it, they need only be told that the water has to soak way down deep into the soil if the roots are to grow down deep where they can get food.

The matter of weeding is something else. Most children think this great sport—for perhaps a single ten-minute session. Weeding fades fast as an attraction,

especially when the gardener is faced with several long rows choked with intruders which must be dispatched (a good reason for making rows short). It becomes a matter of self-interest to use as much mulch as you can to cut down on weeds.

It also pays to give the youngsters a hand with weeding in the early stages, not only for moral support but to help them sort out the unwanted from the wanted. You might also keep in mind that weeds, too, have names and can be identified and studied. In fact, an excellent way to keep interest up and weeds down is to establish a log book through the summer of the kinds of weeds found growing in the garden, the date of their appearance, and a pressed specimen of each. Such garden diaries make enormously interesting personal reference books and good source material when you are playing detective, trying to learn the identity of an uninvited newcomer to the garden.

MAKING MORE FROM ONE

Children will find the whole matter of plant reproduction a fascinating one. From one healthy plant they can make as many as ten to twenty new plants—a good way to multiply their plant holdings and the sort of something-from-nothing, get-rich-quick activity that appeals to children.

The really interesting thing about making more from one as far as children are concerned, though, is the view they get of a form of reproduction not possible in the animal kingdom. Without getting tangled up in a large dose of biology and botany, it is easy enough for them to understand that this method of reproduction is called asexual.

While plants, like animals, are capable of reproducing themselves by sexual means (the result being the seed the child is accustomed to planting), plants can also reproduce asexually (by means other than sex). One can take a leaf or a stem from a plant and from it grow a whole new plant. Rather akin to using the finger of a person to grow another new person exactly like the first. And with that somewhat grisly thought, here are two ways to make more from one.

Making More from One—Indoors

BY THE LEAF, AS WITH AFRICAN VIOLETS

With a sharp knife cut the leaves from a mature plant, taking stems an inch or more long. These can be rooted in one of several different ways:

Try the peat-pot way. Soak a peat disk in water to make a peat pot. (See Getting Started Indoors, page 53.) Poke a small hole in the center of each peat pot, and tuck in the stem of a leaf. Press the soil around the stem. Now either place the pots in a tray and keep them moist, or—and this is neat-looking—collect baby-food jars or other types of containers about the same size, and tuck each planted peat pot up into the jar, leaf first, and then screw the lid back on. The jars, lid–end down and leaf sticking up, can make a whole trayful of miniature terrariums. When new baby plants appear—it will be a number of weeks—remove the peat pot from the jar carefully and transfer to a permanent pot.

Or fill a small glass or jar with water, cover the top with a layer of waxed paper, secure the paper to the top of the glass or jar with a rubber band. Or cut a circle of cardboard a little larger all around than the top of the jar to act as a lid that rests on top of the glass. Then with an ice pick, poke a hole in the top of the waxed

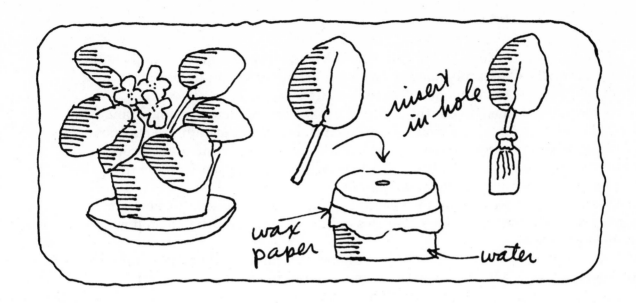

insert in hole

wax paper

water

paper or cardboard and insert the leaf stem, letting the leafy part rest on the top surface and the stem reach into the water on the underside.

Or collect small bottles such as the kind used for individual coffee creamers or the small baby-aspirin bottles. Stand one leaf up in each water-filled bottle and place the bottles on a tray. The trayful of leaves will make an attractive forest of green during the wait for new roots to form.

Keep the water level up as needed. The first roots to form on the stem will be tiny hairlike ones; wait until a few larger roots appear (five or six roots an inch or so long) before transplanting the leaf to its own pot. Now comes another waiting spell and then the great fun of African-violet propagation.

Up from the base of the single leaf will come a whole family of tiny leaves. A complete miniature plant simply pops out. This is the moment when African violets are at their most enchanting. The cluster of leaves—four or five or more—appear all at once. They are tiny as can be, but perfectly shaped and a lovely new green. Children are delighted to be in on the birth of this new little plant and parents will be, too.

Start your leaf cuttings by late summer at least to have small charming plants ready for giving by Christmastime. At this point, you might want to take off the parent leaf and leave the baby plant to shine on its own.

As for the containers to put them in, don't make the mistake of using a fancy enameled or glazed pot for the violet. They do much better in the ordinary clay pots, helped by the porous nature of the clay which allows some air to circulate through the soil. Red clay pots are attractive enough in their own right, especially in this day of basics. Use small ones for small plants.

Young children are usually firmly wedded to the wrapping of gifts, however, so a colored foil for putting around the sides of the pot and a ribbon to hold it will probably be in order.

Even very young children can help in almost any phase of this type of making more from one—with a bit of assistance when it comes to handling the plant because the leaves are tender and somewhat brittle.

Making More from One—Outdoors

BY LAYERING, AS WITH AZALEAS

Layering is best begun in the spring and the new plant separated from the parent in early fall. Layering is a good way to get a really good-sized new plant fast, and children seldom fail to be impressed by the feat. They will enjoy, too, learning the techniques of layering, which are really quite simple.

There are two methods: ground layering and air layering.

Ground layering is particularly suitable for azaleas and rhododendrons. Sometimes these plants will do the layering on their own. If they don't, you can help them along.

From the previous year's growth, choose a low branch of the parent shrub, one that spreads out on the ground or near enough so that it can be bent to touch the ground. Then prepare a shallow narrow trench in the ground below this branch.

Fill the trench with peat moss and water till damp. Then bend the branch into the trench so that it comes in contact with the peat moss. Along the place on the branch where this contact is made, gently scrape off the outer layer of bark, or "skin." Lay this part of the branch onto the moss, and cover with more moss. Now place a good-sized rock over the spot to pin the branch firmly in place in the trench.

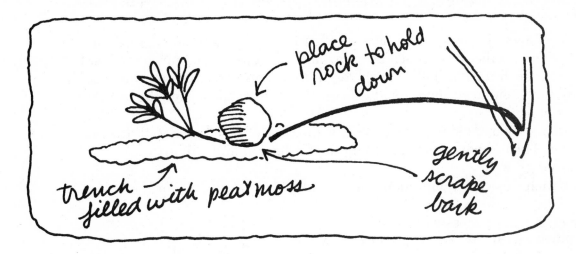

Check to see that the area stays moist over the next several weeks while the new roots begin to form along the branch. When the branch begins to put on new growth, it is a good sign that the layering project is successful. Now the branch can be cut away from the parent plant and settled in a new home of its own.

For air layering, the root forming is done above ground rather than in the ground. You will need some milled sphagnum moss (available in garden stores), which is just like ordinary sphagnum moss, except that it is much finer. It will provide a good sterile medium for the new roots. You will also need some hormone rooting powder such as Rootone or a hormone spray (also available in garden stores). Have on hand a 6-inch square of plastic wrap, electrician's plastic tape and a sharp pocket knife.

Now to the work. First, let the sphagnum moss soak up as much water as it will, then drain off the excess. Select a branch of the previous year's growth of the shrub or tree you want to air layer and locate a spot just below the point (called a node) where a leaf or smaller branch grows. Cut just through the bark all around the parent branch at the node. Then about an inch further down on the branch, again cut all around, taking care not to cut any deeper than just through the outer bark or skin of the branch.

Then peel away the outer skin between the two cuts. This is called 'girdling" the branch. On a smaller plant, such as an azalea, this girdling can be done just by scraping away the branch's skin. The glucose that the plant or tree normally makes for food will now tend to accumulate at this girdle and will encourage the formation of new roots here.

As soon as the outer skin is peeled away, dust the exposed area with the hormone powder. The hormone helps guard against infection and will also encourage root growth.

Now bunch the wet sphagnum moss around the entire girdle. Form a ball of it around the branch and squeeze out excess water. Cover the damp moss with the square of plastic wrap and seal the edges with the electrician's tape where the wrap comes into contact with the branch, making a waterproof seal. The little plastic-wrap pouch will allow you to watch the developing roots as they form, undisturbed by the elements. When there appears to be a good supply of roots, the parent branch may be cut off just below the new root package, the plastic wrap gently removed, and the new plant potted or transplanted to another garden spot.

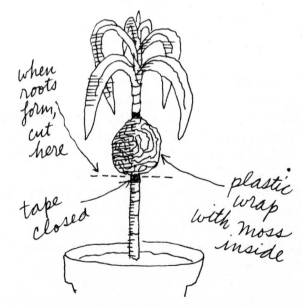

when roots form, cut here

tape closed

plastic wrap with moss inside

74

3 *What to Do Until the Seeds Come Up*

DISCOVERING SECRETS IN THE SEED

After the seeds are planted comes the waiting. But just because all is quiet on the surface of the flower pot or seed bed doesn't mean that plenty isn't going on underground. Now is a good time to look into some of the secrets of the seed while waiting for the ones you have planted to come up.

As a matter of fact, why should seeds come up at all? Why not down? Or sideways? And what about the roots? Is there a pattern in their underground growth? Everyone "knows" that plants bend toward the light and that roots seem to seek water, but when children can see this action focused—a bean plant that will not be denied its place in the sun, a radish root unerringly finding the water—it is a wonder all over again.

A low, fervent "Gee whiz" may be the only outward sign you'll have that a young mind has just had its first glimpse of one of these strange, mysterious forces that govern his universe. That's the reaction that is usually evoked by a tropism happening—plants exhibiting their built-in responses to light, to water, to touch, to gravity.

Many kids will no doubt come upon tropisms as part of a science class in junior high or high school. But by then, there's a difference: at fourteen they have to learn about them; at four they can discover them.

Tropism experiments are easy to set up, observe, and study at home. Bean and radish seeds are among the best to use for seeing tropisms at work. They both germinate easily and quickly. Beans have roots and stems that are large enough to be seen during the tropism, and the seeds themselves are big enough for small children to handle easily. (If you soak them in water overnight they'll germinate even faster.)

And if you use a regular green bean variety (a pole type, not a bush) in some of your tropism gardening, the plants may go long enough to give the children a green bean or two—sometimes many more—to munch on. (And let them eat them raw—they're good that way.) Or the beans can, of course, provide the seeds of yet another tropism garden; and there's something to be absorbed here, too—this endless chain from seed to plant to seed again.

Seeds come up, of course, in response to the sun. You can isolate and dramatize this action, known as a heliotropism, with a glass jar, paper toweling and a half dozen radish seeds.

Roll a length of paper toweling around a glass jar, then cut it to fit the jar's height and circumference. Rinse out the glass jar with water—don't dry it—and then line it with the paper toweling. Add about an inch of water to the jar.

Now slip the radish seeds between the jar and toweling, spaced in a single row about an inch below the rim of the jar. They're small and may be devilish to arrange with your fingers—so use a toothpick.

Put the jar in a dark place and leave undisturbed so that the seeds will not be able to get a peek at the sun and know which way is up. At night, shine in a flashlight to take a peek at the seeds from time to time, and when the stems are up about an inch, take the jar out, pour off the water and put the jar back in place. But *this* time, turn the jar on its side (which is why you pour off the water!).

After a few more days of growth, take a look at the plants again and you will see that they have made a left turn from the horizontal position they were in when

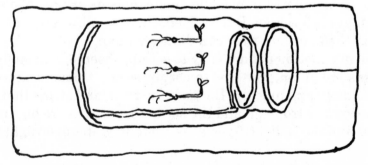

the jar was put on its side, and the plants are now headed up again. If you keep on with the experiment, adding just a bit of soluble fertilizer to the water to keep the plant nourished (when the jar is in an upright position, the stem will soon look like stairsteps climbing toward the sun. Yes, seeds know which way is up.

Another tropism in response to light, not necessarily sunlight, is called phototropism, and is easy to demonstrate, too. You will need a shoe box with a lid, enough garden soil to fill it almost to the top and about two cups of gravel. Cut an inch or so out of one end of the box from the top down and then line the box with aluminum foil. Place a layer of gravel in the bottom of the box for drainage, add the soil, and then water till damp but not soaking. Now plant whatever seed you have on hand. Beans are fine.

Put the lid on the box, and place it on a windowsill, and tell yourself and the kids "no peeking" for at least a week.

After a week, open the lid just long enough to add water to moisten the soil again. The beans may be up—probably are—but don't leave the lid off for long. Just water and put the lid right back on.

In another week comes the unveiling. Off with the lid. All of the plants will be up and growing now, and with no one to tell them which way the light is and no eyes to see with, still there the little bean plants are, all bending toward the patch of light at the end of the box. Bean plants are smart. All plants are smart. They know. They know.

A sweet potato also makes a smart phototropism performer. Make a maze

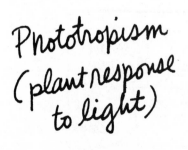

Phototropism (plant response to light)

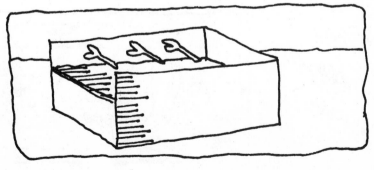

from a shoe box by adding a three-quarter partition to one side of the box and another three-quarter partition to the other side of the box. Cut out one end of the box as described above. Put a small sweet potato in a small glass of water and place it in one end of the box and put the lid on. As the plant grows, it will wind its way toward the light at the other end of the box. You can peek every so often to see how far it has come along.

Now what about the roots? A demonstration of a geotropism—a plant's movement in response to gravity—will show a curious youngster what goes on underground.

Two small sheets of glass are often recommended for this tropism demonstration, but a clear plastic envelope, such as a page from a photo album, works perfectly and is easier for the child to handle.

You will be making a plastic sandwich with a layer of paper toweling and seeds in between the two plastic sides. Fold or cut two or three layers of paper toweling to the proper size to fit inside the plastic envelope. Place inside and hold the open edge of the envelope under the water tap with just a fine stream of water until the paper toweling is saturated; pat the outside of the envelope dry.

Now, lifting up one side of the envelope, reach in and place the seeds on the paper, in a straight row along one side, a couple of inches in from the edge and a couple of inches apart. After you have the seeds arranged on the toweling, you can hang the envelope by a clothespin to a convenient anything—towel rack, curtain rod, clothesline. In a few days you will see the roots growing. They will be pointed

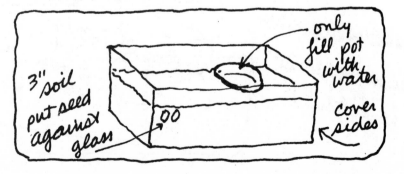

Hydrotropism (plant response to water)

3" soil put seed against glass

only fill pot with water

cover sides

down—just as all good roots should. (If you use a colored paper towel rather than a white one the roots will show up much better.) After the roots have grown an inch or so, turn the envelope around so that what was the top is down and the former bottom is up. Wait a couple of days and check the roots again. You had pointed the roots up but now you will see they are headed back down again.

If you watch the roots carefully and catch them at the right length each time, by hanging the envelope up, down, sideways, and from points in between, you can create your own design. Keep the toweling moist throughout by adding water in just a small trickle from the tap or spooned in over the toweling.

You may be successful in having the roots spell out an initial for you during its process of always seeking to send its roots down toward the earth. Figuring out which way to turn the sandwich and when, in order to come up with the right pattern, can be tricky but lots of fun. An "S" for Sue is a cinch; but a "B" for Bill isn't all that easy!

Probably the most fascinating tropism for children to work with, the most mysterious and the most dramatic, is a hydrotropism—a plant's movement in response to water.

You will need a clear plastic or glass container for this tropism demonstration. A plastic shoe box, a refrigerator container, an aquarium or any other clear glass container that is at least 8 inches or so long and 3 inches or so deep will do.

Fill the container with about 3 inches of soil, and add only enough water to moisten it. At one end bury a small clay flowerpot (with its drainage hole taped

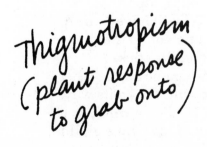

Thigmotropism (plant response to grab onto)

start with small stick

add taller & taller sticks

81

closed) in the soil up to its rim. The porous clay pot will allow some moisture, but not a whole lot at a time, to come through the sides. Now plant seeds at the opposite end of the container, up against the clear glass front so that you can see the action when roots begin to grow. Any type of seed that you have on hand will work, but melon seeds are flattish and are generally off to a fast start.

Now cover the sides of the container so that no light can enter. Tape newspaper or roll foil around the edges, so that it will be easy to open up and peek at what's going on underground when the time comes.

Add water only to the flowerpot and not anywhere else. In a few days, check to see if the roots have emerged and which way they are headed. 'Twill be toward the clay pot of water. Plants can sniff out, feel out, somehow just sense where the water is and they will go for it. This built-in sensor helps plants to survive in periods of drought.

Thigmotropism. From the moment the kids hear about this one, it becomes "thing-ama-tropism." Well, no matter, but just for the record, thigmo comes from the Greek word for "touch," and some plants show this tropism very clearly by reaching out to grab on to whatever comes close to them. And they can sense that "something" is there to grab on to—without eyes to see, yet! So thigmotropism gardens become a sort of plants' version of Blind Man's Bluff (or is it Buff?).

For a thigmotropic garden, use bean seeds, or cucumber, which will also put on a highly thigmotropic show. Plant the seeds in a pot. (See The ABC's of Gardening, page 53.)

When the seeds first sprout, sink a short stick (12 inches high) into the pot to one side of the plants. After the true leaves (the second pair of leaves) have formed, and the plant takes off growing, it will put out tendrils. These latch on to the stick and curl around it, and the plant itself twines around and around the stick.

When the plant has reached the top of the stick, place a taller one on the other side of the pot. The plant will shift its growth to that stick and continue on its way. Make its next step a string—stretched from the stick out to the cord on a window shade, say. The bean plant will happily follow along. (Needless to say, while all this is going on, no more pulling the shade up and down, so if that's a must, entice your bean plant elsewhere.)

    With several plants growing, and some string, a youngster can create an intricate leafy green bower in his own bedroom. If there is not sufficient light from the windows, a small tabletop grow light on the pots themselves can help produce a small harvest of beans.

FOLLOWING FAMOUS SCIENTISTS

    Most would-be gardeners accept without question the fact that green growing plants need soil, water, air and sunshine. They are happy to have helpful hints wrapped up in chapters such as What Every Good Gardener Should Know.

    It is the young and growing green gardener who is most likely to ask

"Why?" and "How come?" "If we get all our food from plants, where do plants get *their* food?"

The answers for many such questions can be found in the lives of people who have enriched our own lives through their devotion to the green world. A fascinating journey awaits anyone who troubles to look into the lives of some of the famous scientists and naturalists of the past. Your child will not only find answers to questions, but by following these famous green people, a kinship develops—a deep satisfaction that comes from knowing that their interests in the world around them today are anchored not to passing fads or trendy styles but to concerns that span all the years that man has inquired into and revered the living, growing things around him.

Van Helmont, Hales, Priestley

So where do plants get their food? Three of the "food factory" scientists can tell you.

Aristotle, who lived three-hundred and fifty years before Christ, believed that plants got their food from the soil in which they were rooted. No one thought to actually test this idea until the early part of the seventeenth century when a Belgian scientist, Jean Baptiste van Helmont, set up an experiment to do so. He planted a young willow tree weighing 5 pounds in a container which held exactly 200 pounds of soil. After five years of tending the tree, van Helmont uprooted it, carefully removed the soil from its roots and weighed the tree. It had gained 164 pounds, 3 ounces. Then van Helmont weighed the soil. It weighed almost the same as it had five years earlier—200 pounds, less 2 ounces. "Aha," van Helmont must have said to himself, "the weight that the tree gained must have come from something besides the soil—at least all but 2 ounces of it came from somewhere else." He concluded that it came from the only other thing he had added over the five years: water.

About a hundred years later, an English clergyman, Stephen Hales, studied the way that water moved through plant roots, up through the branches and to the leaves. But since the water did not seem to accumulate in or drip from the leaves, Hales reasoned that the leaves of the plant must give off water *to* the air and take nourishment in *from* the air.

Then another Englishman, Joseph Priestley, performed, in 1772, some dramatic experiments to see if plants *could* breathe as Hales had suggested. He placed a burning candle inside a jar, and it burned itself out in only a few minutes. When he placed a mouse in a closed jar, it soon died. Priestley concluded that the candle and the mouse somehow had "damaged" the air. So when he put a sprig of mint in a glass of water and placed it in the same jar in which some of his laboratory mice had died, he was surprised to see the plant did not die as he had expected but seemed to thrive instead. He concluded that somehow the plant "repaired" the air

man needs plants to purify the air—

that the mice had damaged. "Plants tend to keep the atmosphere sweet and wholesome," he wrote, and in doing so he put his finger on an interaction between the plant and animal kingdoms that is basic to the science of ecology: mice and every other animal, including man, need plants to purify the air.

In the years that followed, the work of other scientists slowly added to what we know today:

● That van Helmont's willow tree did gain two ounces of its weight from the soil—from minerals in the soil which are dissolved by the water, enabling them to be absorbed by the roots of the plant.

● That the movement of water through a plant, as Hales had observed, is necessary to the plant's food-making process.

● That Priestley's mice died because they had "breathed up" all the oxygen in the jar while breathing out carbon dioxide; and that the mint plant lived because it breathed in the carbon dioxide that the mice had breathed out.

● That the leaves of green plants are actually "food factories" where water, carbon dioxide from the air, and sunlight interact in a process called photosynthesis to make simple sugar that is the plant's food and at the same time release life-sustaining oxygen into the air.

● And the final answer to that puzzler of where plants get their food: that they make it themselves from the substances about them—soil, water, air and sunlight.

You can easily duplicate van Helmont's experiment by weighing the soil and container in which you put a young plant. Five years would be a long time to wait before checking results, though. Settle for five months instead, and then see how much weight your plant has gained.

VAN HELMONT'S EXPERIMENT

PLANT GROWTH CHART

date	height or length of plant	weight of plant	weight of container & soil	new developments

YOUR GROWTH CHART

date	height	weight

Weigh yourself at the beginning and end of the experiment, too. Did you gain more weight than your plant? Did you gain more weight *proportionately* than your plant? Remember for the last answer compare your weight gain against your own previous weight—not against the plant's weight gain. If the plant weighed 4 ounces when the experiment began, for example, and now weighs a pound, it would have quadrupled its weight. Did you quadruple your weight? Not likely!

As for Hales' notion of water moving up through the plant, you can see a plant's water pipes for yourself.

Select a stalk of celery with a good leafy top. Cut off an inch from the bottom and put the remainder of the stalk in a glass of water to which you have added food coloring. (To half a glass or more of water, add enough coloring to turn the water a deep dark color; red works best. Less than half a glass of water makes a stronger solution and requires less coloring.) Put the glass in bright light. It won't be long—a half hour—and you will see the celery leaves at the top beginning to

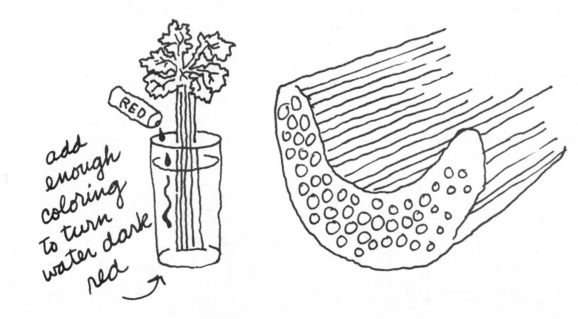

add enough coloring to turn water dark red

change color; a reddish-brown tinge will spread through them, or blue-green if you have used blue coloring.

To see how the coloring got from the bottom of the stalk to the top, take the celery out of the glass and cut another half-inch off the end of the stalk. You will see pinpoints of red coloring all around the edge of the celery. These are the "tubes" that send the water up through the plant.

Take a knife and gently scrape along the celery stalk. As you remove the outer layer of the stalk, you can see the colored tubes running all the way along the length of the stalk. (You can eat the rest of the experiment.) Now you also know how florists are able to make green carnations for St. Patrick's Day; next time you have some white flowers you can experiment with them to see if they will "take" another color.

You might also want to try an experiment similar to Priestley's (with the candle, not the mouse!). In a small glass of water put a sprig of mint or other plant that will live in water—ivy, for example—and cover the whole thing with a large jar. A big-size, wide-mouthed, peanut butter jar is good. Place the jar where it will receive some sunlight every day and leave it undisturbed.

Plan to have on hand a second identical jar and two birthday candles. At the end of ten days (during which time the plant in the first jar will be breathing out oxygen) light one birthday candle, stand it up in a drop of hardened wax and invert the second jar over it. Time how long it takes before the candle goes out. Then light the second candle and place it in the jar with the plant. Time how long the candle will burn there.

leave for 10 days

now see which burns longer!

90

Carolus Linnaeus
(1701-1778)

As you look through your seed catalogs, you may be puzzled (or impressed) by some of the Latin or Latinized words following the English names for the plants. The Latin name is the formal name of a plant—one that identifies it to plant scientists all over the world.

Throughout history, man has felt compelled to label things—to give some kind of name to every different thing he encounters. Scientists struggled for centuries trying to sort plants in some kind of order, trying one system and then another. But all was mostly chaos, with some plants having names eight or nine words long, until the young Swedish botanist Carolus Linnaeus, also known as Carl von Linne, boldly decided that specific plants need have only two names (a binomial system) and that all plants could be grouped into large families according to the similarities of their reproductive parts.

Such an idea was something of a shocker at the time, for plant scientists had not considered that there might be sexual differences among plants. But Linnaeus went on to classify and describe thousands and thousands of different plants, producing in the process more than 185 books. In one book alone, his famous *Species Plantarum,* he described more than 7300 plants, most of which he had classified and illustrated himself and had represented in his own herbarium (special files for preserving plant materials).

You will find that a do-it-yourself classification of plants can make a great family activity—maybe for some vacation evening after a day of fun in the outdoors. Beforehand, collect twigs with leaves attached from a number of different trees.

Lay your leaves out in front of you so that you can look at them all carefully. What you will be doing is playing a sort of Twenty Questions—how are the twigs and leaves alike, and how are they different?

Have pencil and paper on hand so you can make a diagram as you go. Here are some questions to get you started:

1. Is the foliage needlelike or scalelike? Or is it broad and leafy? The answers immediately give you your first two classifications: (a) needlelike or scalelike foliage, and (b) broad and leafy foliage.
2. Is the foliage in 1(a) above needlelike? Is it scalelike? You now have two more classifications.
3. Are the broad leaves in 1(b) above in one piece (a simple leaf)? Are some of them made up of leaflets (compounds)? Here are two more classifications.

From making a seemingly very simple classification job involving only a few twigs and leaves you will wind up fascinated at the absolutely incredible amount of work Linnaeus did—observing, describing, classifying, illustrating thousands of plants, not only their leaves and twigs but their flowers, fruit, seeds and many, many other details.

The diagram (pg.94) will suggest more questions to help you classify your collection further.

You will also find it fun to learn the Latin names for a few of your plants. And once you know only a few, botanical names no longer seem quite so complicated. Also, you can say you have an *Ipomoea batatas* growing on your windowsill if you think your sweet potato lacks class.

Look at this list, for example:

Quercus alba L.	White oak
Quercus rubra L.	(Northern) Red oak
Acer rubrum L.	Red maple
Acer nigrum	Black maple
Populus alba L.	White poplar

If you know the word *Quercus,* you know the first name of all the oaks; *Acer,* all the maples; *Populus,* you can guess. The words *alba, rubrum, nigrum* (white, red, black), or variations, describe the trees—whether maple, oak or other plants. There are many other descriptive Latin or Latinized words that you will be able to guess easily: *pyrimidata, grandiflora, magnifica, Americana,* to mention a few. And any botanical name with an *L.* after it means that the plant was described and classified by Linnaeus himself, who even Latinized his own name while he was at it.

Here are the Latin and common names for ten vegetables that might come from your own garden. See if you can match them up. If you're stumped, check the dictionary:

1. *Solanum tuberosum*
2. *Cucumis sativus*
3. *Raphanus sativus*
4. *Lycopersicon esculentum*
5. *Allium cepa*
6. *Brassica rapa*
7. *Zea mays*
8. *Lactuca sativa*
9. *Beta vulgaris*
10. *Spinacia oleracea*

1. Lettuce
2. Beet
3. Tomato
4. Turnip
5. Corn
6. Radish
7. Spinach
8. Cucumber
9. Onion
10. Potato

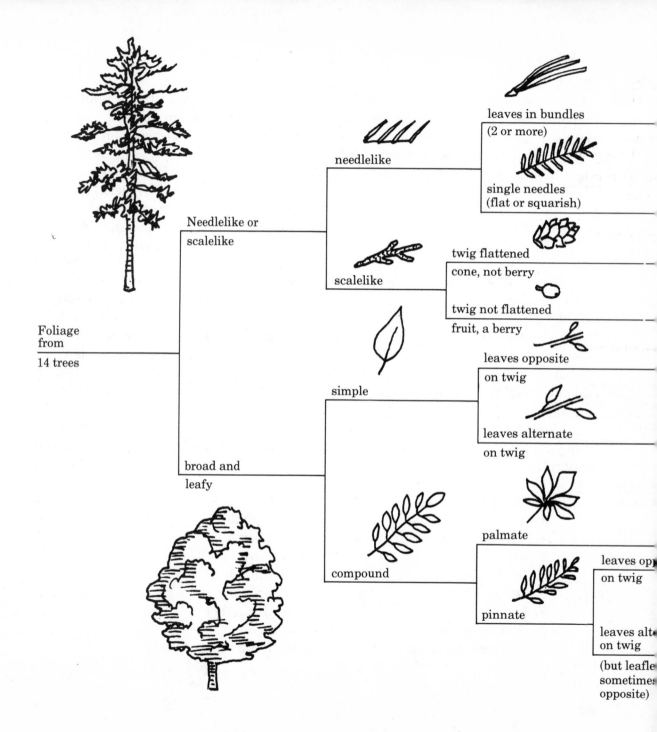

Foliage
from
14 trees

Needlelike or
scalelike

needlelike

leaves in bundles
(2 or more)

single needles
(flat or squarish)

scalelike

twig flattened
cone, not berry

twig not flattened
fruit, a berry

broad and
leafy

simple

leaves opposite
on twig

leaves alternate
on twig

compound

palmate

pinnate

leaves op
on twig

leaves alt
on twig

(but leafle
sometime
opposite)

ndles of 5 needles
o 5 inches long ———————————————————————— WHITE PINE

ndles of 3 needles
o 10 inches long
——————————————————————— LOBLOLLY PINE
ached to twig
——————————————————————— HEMLOCK
short stalk

thout stalk ———————————————————————— SPRUCE
————————————————————————————— ARBORVITAE

——————————————————————————— JUNIPER
f margin ———————————————————————— MAPLE
othed or lobed

f margin not ———————————————————————— DOGWOOD
othed or lobed ——————————————————————— RHODODENDRON
aves thick,   leaf tip has
athery, evergreen   wide, shallow ———— TULIP TREE
                    leaf deeply   notch
                    lobed
aves deciduous
ft, thin

——————————————————————————— BUCKEYE
———————————————————————— ASH
stems on twigs ——————————————————— LOCUST
thorny

stems on twigs ————————————————— HICKORY
not thorny

95

Charles Darwin (1809-1882)

Charles Darwin is best known for his scientific explanation of evolution—all the phenomena of life related in one comprehensive theory—which he described in his famous book, *The Origin of Species*. But Darwin's fascination with all aspects of nature also produced an enormous amount of work devoted especially to plants: insect-eating plants, plant movement (see the section on tropisms, pg. 77), plant seeds and how they are distributed from place to place. He was, in fact, especially fond of plants, once writing, "It has always pleased me to exalt plants in the scale of organized beings."

He talked about his plants in personal terms, too. "The little beggars are doing just what I don't want them to do," he complained about a group of seedlings he was observing.

Today, you hear of experiments to determine if plants respond to music or conversation, or if they can be frightened by such things as a lighted match held near them. To some people, this all seems a bit silly. But it's not likely it would have seemed silly to Charles Darwin. After all, he once played the piano to earthworms! He also blew whistles and shouted at them, breathed on them with a tobacco breath, and held red-hot pokers near them to study their responses.

A scientist whose interests ranged from the possible inheritance of handwriting patterns to the question of whether plants have memories or animals have guilt feelings—yes, such a scientist would be willing to give his plants a dose of rock music to see how they might respond.

Darwin could not play recorded music to his plants, but it would be no disparagement of his accomplishments to design an experiment around the effects of such music on plants.

There are any number of ways you can set up your own experiment. You need only remember to keep all the conditions as nearly alike as you can for all the plants:

- Planting the same kind of seeds at the same time.

- Using the same kind of soil.

- Planting at the same depth.

- Giving each plant the same measured amount of food and water.

- Keeping the amount of light and the rest of the environment the same.

- Having only *one* variable—the music.

Some of your plants will "listen" to music for a certain amount of time each day; others will not be exposed to any music at all. (The latter are called "controls.")

Such an experiment makes a popular science fair project. See if you can design yours with some interesting variations; demonstrating different results, if any, for example, based on the type of music the plants have "heard"—differences among, say, plants that have "listened" to Bach, those that have "listened" to the Beatles, and those (the controls) that have not been exposed to either.

There are many studies of Darwin's that you can duplicate almost exactly. The following two were made by him to demonstrate how plant life can be distributed over widely separated areas. Both will be easy for you to duplicate and as interesting to you as Darwin found them.

In February of one year, Darwin took 3 tablespoons of mud from three different points, beneath water, at the edge of a little pond. He let the mud dry and then weighed it, and found it to weigh 6¾ ounces. He kept the mud in his study for six months, checking to see what kind of plant life would appear, and pulling up and counting each plant as it grew. From this small ball of mud, 537 plants emerged.

You can duplicate this experiment, taking a sample of mud from three different points near the edge of a pond or little stream. When you return home, eliminate enough of the mud until you have 6¾ ounces, so that your finds will be comparable to Darwin's. If you don't have access to a scale that will weigh in ounces (a postal type, for example), then compromise a bit and measure out 6¾ ounces in a measuring cup and use this amount.

Then proceed as Darwin did, keeping careful records of the number and type of plants that emerge. You may not be able to identify each plant by name, in which case you can either make a little sketch of it for your records or press it to keep in a notebook (see Pressing Flowers, page 223). Later, you can try to identify them from library references. Your child may want to share his and your final results with his science class at school. Or use the study as an entry in the school's science fair.

Now for the second experiment. A friend of Darwin's once sent him the leg of a partridge that had been wounded and died. (Darwin was always asking friends and other scientists to send him different types of specimens to study.) A hard ball of earth had adhered to the bird's leg. Darwin carefully removed this ball of earth and found it to weigh 6½ ounces. He watered it and placed it under a glass jar. Eighty-two plants grew from that small ball of earth.

This experiment will be more difficult to duplicate than the first one, especially if you have no friends who send you birds' legs. But how about the seeds that your dog helps to scatter? After a rainy day, scrape the mud from between his toes. Put this mud in a paper cup and slip the cup into a plastic bag. No doubt your dog will be amazed to learn how many seeds he has been toting around.

John Burroughs (1837-1921)

Many public schools across the United States are named for John Burroughs, one of America's best-loved naturalists. He grew up more interested in watching birds and reading poetry than in the work on his father's farm. At seventeen, he turned to teaching to support himself, and spent whatever free time he had watching the small woods' creatures, the flowers, insects and birds and then telling about them in his writings.

Within a few years, he decided to find a country place of his own where he could spend all of his time observing nature and writing. He bought a nine-acre site along the Hudson, not too far from his boyhood home in Roxbury, New York, and built a house there called Riverby. He planted berries, grapes and other fruits and marketed the produce to support himself.

The building of his own home was one of the greatest pleasures of his life. Gathering the stone for the house, and doing a good part of the construction himself, Burroughs said that "every load carried my heart and happiness with it."

Before long, though, Burroughs had a growing family of his own, and he again felt the need for a more remote place in which to work. Near Riverby, he discovered a setting for a rustic hideaway where he could observe nature undisturbed. There he built a little cabin made mostly from rough slabs cut from logs. A neighbor dubbed it Slabsides. Burroughs later remarked, "Blessed Slabsides! It is indeed a house of refuge to me."

It was at Slabsides that John Burroughs wrote many of his articles and books on nature. Look for *Locusts and Wild Honey, Signs and Seasons, Wake Robin,* and *The Ways of Nature* next time you visit your library.

If you are following John Burroughs, you would enjoy having a hideaway of your own, too. You can, in fact, *grow* your own summer retreat. It might be a nature observatory one day, a fort the next day, even a clubhouse.

A start can be made on your "Greensides" from just a few rough boards or an old packing crate. If you can find four boards to drive in the ground as corner posts, you're in business. Additional boards will help later on for bracing as the green sides and top grow.

Cover the sides and top of the space you have staked out with chicken wire or any kind of old screening, leaving a small entry space at one side. Then, as soon as all danger of frost has passed, plant gourd seeds (see Great Gourd Fun, page 142) or pumpkin seeds (see Pumpkin Derby, page 138). Plant 3 or 4 seeds to a hill at each corner post. Planted in May, the vines will grow quickly and should cover the entire structure by August. You'll find this outdoor hideaway a cool retreat in summer, and a neat place to survey and work on your gourd crop growing within a hand's reach.

You can also grow your outdoor retreat in tepee style. Find three long stakes, poles or boards. Lash them together at the top and anchor the other ends firmly into the ground. Plant either gourd or bean seeds around the base, leaving an opening for you to creep inside after the vines have grown to enclose the tepee frame.

Luther Burbank (1849-1926)

"I wonder if there are really two things in this world which are exactly alike." This was a question that a young boy named Luther Burbank asked himself, and the search for its answer was to be his life's work.

He spent many hours in the fields near his home, studying the oxeye daisies which grew there, trying to find two exactly alike. Although he studied hundreds of them, he could always find slight differences in each one—sometimes in the shape, sometimes in the size or in the color.

Luther Burbank also learned as a boy how to graft plants, connecting the cut ends of two plants together in such a way that they grow to form one plant. In this way, apples have been made to grow on pear trees and pears on apple trees.

In one of his most unusual grafting experiments, he put potato and tomato plants together in two different ways. He first cut off the top of a tomato plant and grafted it onto a potato plant. Then he cut the top of a potato plant and grafted it onto a tomato plant. He got some surprising results! The plant with the potato top

100

and tomato bottom produced some strange growths above ground which were neither potatoes nor tomatoes, and no fruits underground. The plant with the tomato top and potato bottom produced normal tomatoes above ground, but small, misshapen potatoes underground.

During his lifetime, Burbank developed thousands of different types of plants and became internationally known as the Plant Wizard. You might want to try some of the wizardry that Burbank performed, even his potato-tomato plant graft, and see what results *you* obtain. (Not so simple as it sounds, though— Burbank repeated some of his experiments thousands of times before he was satisfied with the results.)

A good plant to work with for a first try at grafting would be the cactus. It is among the easiest to graft. Cacti can also produce some weird combinations. The professional florist or the expert gardener might consider some of these creations too far out, but that is precisely why lots of young gardeners think cactus grafting a neat occupation.

The easiest grafts to make are with the fat, columnar types of cacti. You simply take two of them, lop off their heads and switch tops with each other.

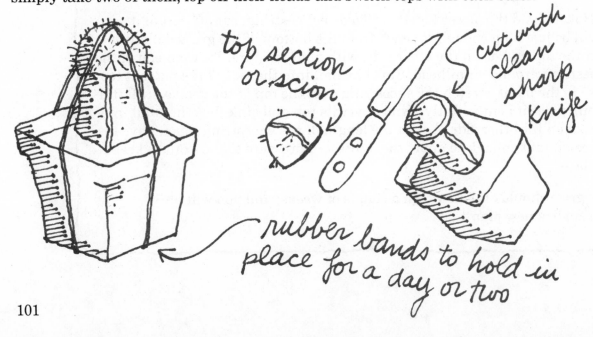

top section or scion

cut with clean sharp knife

rubber bands to hold in place for a day or two

Some pointers:

1. Make grafts during summer months, when plants are growing.

2. Use a good sharp knife.

3. Make as perfectly flat a cut as you can so that the top (the scion) of the one plant will fit as smoothly and completely as possible on the bottom (the stock) of the other.

4. Have everything ready so that after the cut you can make the switch at once.

5. Press the two pieces as gently yet firmly together as possible.

6. Now the important thing is to keep the parts together and undisturbed—not jarring them in the least or letting any water touch the grafting site.

7. How to hold the pieces together? Take a shoestring; cut off part of it so it will be just long enough to reach from the bottom of the grafted plant over the top and down the other side, with a bit to spare. Tie each end of the shoestring around a nailhead. Sink one nail into the side of the pot, not too close to the plant; stretch the shoestring over the top of the cactus graft (the scion); place it gently, flatly, firmly over its top and sink the other nail into the pot on the other side. Adjust the length of the shoestring if you have to to keep it taut enough to apply the lightest of pressure to the graft to keep it in place.

The graft should "take" within a couple of weeks, and you will have "created" a new plant!

George Washington Carver (1864?-1943)

On a winter evening during the Civil War in a little cabin near Diamond Grove, Missouri, a frail black baby was born. His mother, Mary, was a slave owned by a German farmer named Moses Carver. His father, also a slave, was killed in a farm accident shortly after George was born.

When George was only a few weeks old, night riders swooped down on the Carver place and carried off Mary and the tiny baby. A posse caught up with the slave stealers and agreed to trade a racehorse for the pair. But the night riders tricked them and rode off with Mary anyway, leaving the infant behind. Such were the beginnings of a man whose life was a testimony to hard work, vision, a good-humored, unshakable commitment and an abiding faith in God.

Though schooling was denied to black children in his hometown in those days, George was determined to get an education. He did. He received a Bachelor of Science degree and a Master of Science degree in Agriculture from Iowa State University. He also became a distinguished artist and an accomplished musician.

Motivated by the needs of Tuskegee Institute (where he worked for forty-seven years), and the poverty of his race, Carver began to *make* what was needed out of what was on hand. His first laboratory was assembled from assorted pots, pans and jars, gleaned from nearby refuse dumps. And in this laboratory, the pioneer chemurgist literally made hundreds of new industrial products from plants.

From soybeans came a "meatloaf," to break the then monotonous Southern diet of corn bread and salad greens.

From the clays of Alabama came paint pigments.

From peanuts came hundreds of products.

You might not want to tackle making synthetic marble from peanut hulls, or paper from the red peanut skins, as Carver did, but you can make "milk" from a handful of peanuts as he did.

Start with a cupful of shelled peanuts. Blend to a fine powder in an electric blender. (If you don't have a blender, chop the peanuts as finely as you can.) Then place in a saucepan over moderate heat for 10 minutes, stirring to keep from scorching.

Now as much oil as possible must be removed. Do this by placing the peanuts on several thicknesses of paper toweling and cover with additional thicknesses and roll with a rolling pin. Replace the toweling as it absorbs the oil. Carver used a food press for this, so it will take some good hard rolling for you to extract most of the oil from the peanuts.

When they reach a dry crumbly stage, return the peanut meal to the saucepan. Add 3 cups of water, a bit at a time, and stir over low heat to blend the meal with the water. Remove from heat, add ½ teaspoon of sugar and a dash of salt. Cool. Strain through a sieve or cheesecloth to remove the solid peanut meal, and you will have a pitcher of good nutritious peanut milk. (Use the meal for snacks with crackers.)

From the peanut milk that you have made, it is only a step away to thick milk shakes. Back to the blender: add ½ cup of the peanut milk to 2 or 3 big scoops of vanilla ice cream. Add 1 teaspoon vanilla extract. Or 1 teaspoon almond extract. You'll have a filling, nutritious, delicious drink!

If you want to branch out and find a use for everything as Carver did, you will have fun making jelly from peach pits! If your family should buy a bushel of peaches, it is definitely peach-pit jelly-making time. Otherwise, stockpile the pits in the freezer until you have accumulated about 1½ quarts (6 cups) of them. Don't wash or scrub the pits because all the bits of fruit that cling to them will add flavor and color to the jelly. The red pits are especially good to use for extra color, but the brown kind gives just as good a taste.

Break open a few of the pits so that the nutlike seed can add its mild almond flavor to the jelly. Put all the pits in a pan, with water enough to cover (about 2 cups) and simmer for a half hour.

Then strain off the juice. (Save the pits for your mulch bag, your bonsai tray, your seed-study collection, etc. This is a "don't waste anything" exercise!)

Now the juice can be strained through a jelly bag. You can improvise a jelly bag by using a clean white dishtowel. Wet it first and wring it out. Tie all four corners of it around the water faucet in the kitchen sink, put a pan underneath it and carefully pour the juice into the towel and let it drip through to the pan. If you want the very clearest, *clearest* jelly, do not squeeze the bag at all; just let the juice drip slowly through. It will take some time, but a very clear, delicate jelly—the type that wins prizes at fairs—will be the result.

For the last step of the jelly making, you will need ¼ cup of lemon juice, ½ box of pectin and 2¼ cups of sugar for 1¾ cups of the strained juice. Follow the directions for cooking jelly that are given on the pectin box.

Rachel Carson (1907-1964)

If you were asked to choose the one person you thought most responsible for the love and care and concern we are now showing our environment, a good bet would be Rachel Carson. A marine zoologist by training, and a nature lover all her life, Rachel Carson was greatly concerned about the effect of man's technology on the other living things with whom we share our planet earth.

In the book *Silent Spring,* published in 1962, she warned of a spring to come when there would be no birds to sing unless we learned more about the effects of insecticides and other chemicals, not only on birds but on our whole environment. The book received an incredible amount of attention, with some people condemning it and others praising it. It inspired countless studies, investigations, meetings, congressional hearings and new laws—and today we know a great deal more about the intricate relationships of all living things. But more important, we know that we need to know a great deal more.

Rachel Carson, and other scientists before her, thought that one way we might fight insects—better than by chemical methods—was through the use of biological controls, using natural enemies such as other insects to keep destructive pests under control.

You can put this philosophy to work in your own garden. Companion planting—marigolds with your tomatoes, for example—is one way. (See Five-Foot Farm No. 5, page 120.)

Picking off insects you see chewing on your plants rather than running for the spray can is another. (Obviously the use of some biological controls can be much easier for you than for the full-scale farmer! You're only farming a few feet—which also means, of course, that you really have little excuse most of the time for pouring on insecticides.)

As for using good insects against the bad ones, you can set loose two different kinds of farmers' friends to help you protect your garden.

First there is the praying mantis. You can order egg cases of these longlegged, bulgy-eyed critters from mail-order houses, but you may also be lucky enough to find an egg case outdoors, attached to the branch of a bush or on a flower stalk.

The cases are light-brown puffs about the size of a golf ball. Each case contains hundreds of eggs. When the baby mantis emerges it is not much bigger than a mosquito, and it will be five or six months till it grows to full size.

You won't get a chance to see the praying mantis emerge unless you keep the egg case indoors. The whole thing happens quickly. When the time is right, the mantises are up and out of the egg case within an hour. They crawl up out of a slit in the side of the case and let themselves down off of it in a living chain.

If you want the mantises to hatch indoors where you can see them, then keep the case in the refrigerator until two weeks or so before dependably warm weather arrives—the end of April or the first part of May. Then bring the egg case out into room temperature. Be sure to keep it in a jar with a lid on it, with holes punched in the lid, or you might wake up some morning to find that an invasion of small green things has taken over.

You can keep the new mantises in the jar for a couple of days after they hatch to watch them grow, but not any longer than that. They have to be put outside soon because, for one thing, there are so many of them, and also they will be needing insects to eat.

106

Those mantises that survive the hazards of their world will make new egg cases for the young that will follow them next spring.

The egg cases are winter-hardy and can take even sub-zero temperatures, so they can be left outside if indoor mantis hatching doesn't go over as an especially appealing sport at your house.

The more mantises you release the better chance they have of establishing a colony, so two or three cases for your garden would be better than just one.

Ladybugs are also available to help rid your garden of aphids, mealy bugs and other destructive insects. They can be ordered from garden catalogs and will be delivered when the weather is warm. You release them in your garden at the base of the plants you want protected. The birds, of course, will thin the ladybug ranks somewhat, but the little helper bugs will have their whack at some of your garden pests, too.

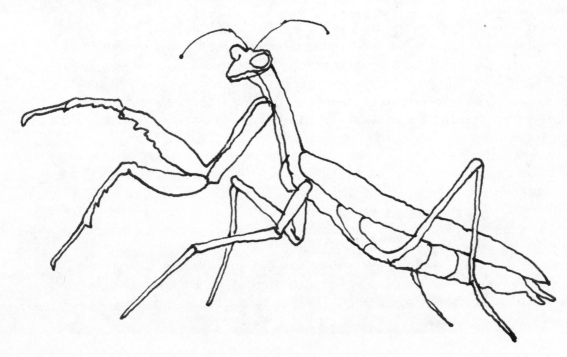

PART TWO GROWING THE GREEN THINGS

4 Gardening for Food & Fun

MINI-FARMING

Gardening of any kind is a rewarding occupation, but if it is at all possible for a child to experience gardening as "farming," he should have that opportunity. No other form of gardening can quite produce the remarkable satisfaction that comes from working with the land and bringing from it food for your own table.

If you have access to a patch of earth that receives at least six, better eight, hours of sunlight a day, then you simply must put in an outdoor garden. No matter if it is only a narrow strip of ground between your apartment entrance and the one next door, it can be producing food—and lots of fun.

In case you are thinking that you haven't enough room for farming, consider what a space five feet by five feet can grow:

Three tomato plants
Two green pepper plants
A five-foot row of lettuce
A five-foot row of beets
A five-foot row of string beans
A five-foot row of carrots
A five-foot row of onions
A five-foot row of radishes

That is enough vegetables to keep the family table supplied for a good part of the summer.

Of course, your farm needn't be limited to five feet, any more than it need be as *much* as five feet.

Now to the planting. Let the children come up with their own arrangement of the garden. In a small plot, efficiency in the care of the crop is not all that important, so who is to say radishes have to be all together in one row? Maybe the children would like to design an arrangement of radishes with lettuce or green onions. Give them some paper and the seed packets and let them design their own. This can be a rewarding winter's day activity. If your child is old enough to mark off inches on the ruler, let him lay out the garden space an inch to the foot, else do it for him. Then from catalogs and other information (even guesses) which you supply, he can draw off the space that each planting will take.

Some children like the tidy, organized approach; others will scatter their crops with abandon. Whichever way, let them draw in their garden plan in the same spirit they would approach any other art—where nobody has to stay "in the lines" if they don't want to. Some might want to design a traditional row garden; others might like a half-dozen radish rosettes in each corner, flanked by leaf lettuce and backed up by a semicircle of straight green onion stalks. Or the whole farm might be devoted to a sunflower jungle or a bean pole tepee or to one type of crop for each child to grow for their own "state fair" competition.

Or they can have a let's-see-what-they-look-like garden, planting crops for which they, and you, have no idea what they look like (not hard to find such plants when a great many of us haven't the foggiest notion of what an eggplant plant looks like). Maybe they will wind up with a "generosity" garden: sunflowers for the birds, catnip for the cat, popcorn for them—and here, of course, try to sneak in at least one tomato plant for you!

And if you are looking forward to table treats yourself, many children are happy with the idea of a salad garden. Or you might suggest a Mediterranean garden, with tomatoes, eggplant, green peppers, Italian squash and onions. Or a Chinese garden, with Chinese celery, cabbage, snowpeas, leeks, white radishes, cucumber, bok choy (a chardlike green) and coriander.

Consider the following five-foot gardens and then come up with variations of your own.

Five-Foot Farm No. 1

LAND OF THE GIANTS

Plant those varieties which will yield giant-size fruits and/or vegetables. Of course, with only five square feet, you will be limited to only one or two of any one kind of these plants. If you are entering a competition to grow the largest pumpkin or largest watermelon, such as is often held at county fairs, you should pick off all the fruit as it appears on the vine with the exception of two or three. These remaining fruits will then grow to a much larger size, since they do not have to compete for moisture. (See also Pumpkin Derby, page 138.) Try these varieties:

Pumpkins:	Big Max (Burpee*, Earl May*). Pumpkins average narly 100 pounds each.
Tomatoes:	Beefmaster (Parks*). Yields tomatoes which weigh up to 2 pounds each. Delicious (Burpee). Average tomato weighs more than 1 pound.
Cabbage:	Hybrid O-S (Burpee, Earl May). Heads weigh up to 20 pounds.
Watermelon:	Black Diamond (Parks, Earl May). Has produced melons up to 125 pounds.

Don't just think big, grow it big, too. Sow your seeds and then get out of the way.

* Seed company addresses: **W. Atlee Burpee Company,** Philadelphia, Pennsylvania 19132; Riverside, California 92502; Clinton, Iowa 52732. **Earl May Seed and Nursery Company,** Shenandoah, Iowa 51601. **Geo. W. Park Seed Company, Inc.,** Greenwood, South Carolina 29646.

Suggested Plot for Circus Garden

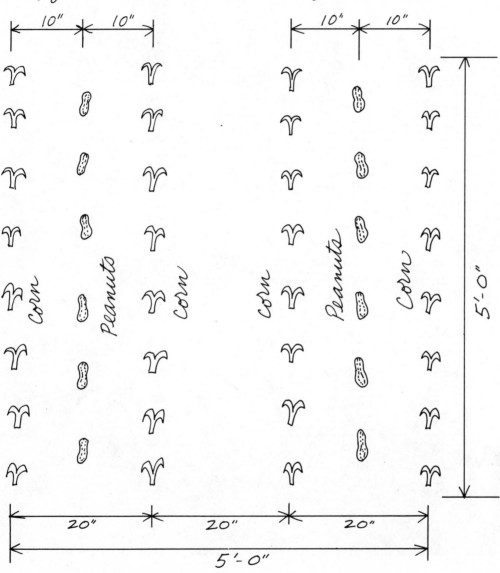

Five-Foot Farm No. 2

A CIRCUS GARDEN

Have you ever thought about having a neighborhood circus? Most youngsters at some time or another, usually just after attending the circus, feel the urge to ascend the high wire, train their pet dog to jump through the hula hoop, or fight off snarling lions (younger brother in old Halloween costume).

So how about growing your own circus refreshments? Peanuts and popcorn, what else?

The peanut is not, of course, really a nut at all, but is a member of the same family as are peas and beans, the legume family. The most popular types are the small Spanish peanut, with 2 to 5 small round nuts in its pod, and the jumbo Virginia peanut, usually with 2 large long nuts in the pod. You cannot raise peanuts from those purchased at the circus because they have been roasted and will not germinate. But sometimes you can buy raw peanuts in the grocery. And you can order them from seed companies.

Once peanuts have been planted, they actually plant themselves for future crops, as you will see when you raise them for yourself. They thrive in a well-drained, loose soil because it gives little resistance to the forming pods. A limited crop can even be raised indoors in hanging baskets. (See Tomatoes in a Basket, page 127.) If you plant them outdoors, wait until all danger of frost is past. They may be planted in the shell, or for quicker germination shell them out. Either way, germination can be speeded up by soaking the peanuts overnight. If you shell them out before planting, be very careful not to damage the thin protective skin over the nuts. If shelled, the large type can be planted about 10 inches apart and the small type about 5 inches apart. Double the spacing if not shelled out, as all the nuts in the pod may sprout. Plant the nuts about 2 inches deep, covering and firming the earth well. For the next couple of weeks the peanuts will be busy making root growth. Then the delicate top growth will appear—a beautiful foliage which later will bear sweet-pea-like yellow blossoms.

As the flowers fade, the plant puts down a long slender spike, sometimes called a peg, which heads straight into the soil and continues to grow until it reaches the "proper" planting depth (1 to 3 inches). This is how the peanut plants itself. The peanut pods will form on these underground shoots. Do not cultivate or hoe around the plants after they send down these pegs, as you may disturb the forming peanuts.

October is usually harvest time. When the leaves begin to turn yellow, usually just before frost, gently loosen the soil around the vines and pull up the entire plant. There will be your peanut crop, hanging just above the tangled roots of the plant. Hang the vines with the peanuts on the roots in a dry airy place for two to three weeks or until the peanuts are well dried. Then you can pick them from the vines.

Most people think roasting peanuts improves their flavor. They can be roasted in the shell or shelled out and then roasted in a flat shallow pan in a thin layer of cooking oil. Roast them slowly for about an hour in a moderate oven (about 300 degrees), stirring occasionally to prevent scorching. Then remove and let cool. Yum yum.

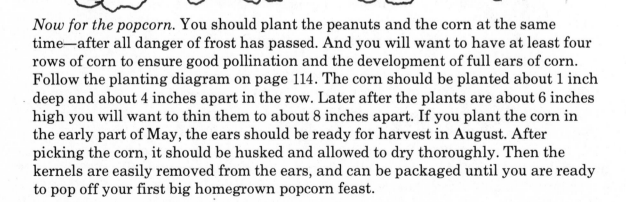

Now for the popcorn. You should plant the peanuts and the corn at the same time—after all danger of frost has passed. And you will want to have at least four rows of corn to ensure good pollination and the development of full ears of corn. Follow the planting diagram on page 114. The corn should be planted about 1 inch deep and about 4 inches apart in the row. Later after the plants are about 6 inches high you will want to thin them to about 8 inches apart. If you plant the corn in the early part of May, the ears should be ready for harvest in August. After picking the corn, it should be husked and allowed to dry thoroughly. Then the kernels are easily removed from the ears, and can be packaged until you are ready to pop off your first big homegrown popcorn feast.

Five-Foot Farm No. 3

IT'S FOR THE BIRDS

A great way to combine the hobbies of gardening and bird-watching is to make a special bird-food farm, planting those goodies that birds dote on. Since water is as important as food in attracting birds to your yard, you may want to plant this farm around a bird bath or fountain.

One of the most popular foods, especially with cardinals and goldfinches, is the seed from sunflowers. This is a very interesting and easily grown plant. Order the Russian Mammoth variety for the largest heads, usually over 12 inches across, supported on 10- to 12-foot stalks. During the growing season the sunflower's practice of turning its head toward the sun as the sun's position shifts in the sky makes it an interesting plant to watch. (A phototropism at work; see page 79 .) At maturity, most of the sunflower heads will be hanging in an east or northeast direction.

Seeds should be planted about 6 inches apart in rows about 2 feet apart. Try the circle arrangement shown here.

Sunflowers with Birdbath at the center

After the sunflowers have bloomed, you will see that the center of each big flower is composed of hundreds of large black seeds. Now is when the red birds and finches will appear to gobble up the goodies. You will enjoy eating them, too. Crack the thin shells with your teeth to find the tasty little "nut" inside. And break off some of the heads to hang upside down in the trees for extra dining places for the birds.

Five-Foot Farm No. 4

LAND OF THE MIDGETS

Over the last few years, seed companies and plant researchers have been busy developing varieties of vegetables with compact growth patterns which make them suitable for growing in containers or in small gardens. They are especially fun for children to grow, harvest and devour. The following varieties are particularly suited for a land-of-the-midgets farm. In five square feet, you can grow at least a sampling of quite a few of these garden goodies:

Beets:	Baby Canning Beet No. 203 (Earl May); Detroit Dark Red (Burpee, Parks).
Cabbage:	Earliana (Burpee); Baby Head Cabbage No. 231 (Earl May); Dwarf Morden (Parks).
Cantaloupe:	Minnesota Midget (Parks); Early Sugar Midget No. 445 (Earl May); Burpee's Netted Gem (Burpee).
Carrots:	Little Finger (Burpee); Tiny Sweet (Parks).
Sweet Corn:	Golden Midget (Burpee, Parks); Midget Sweet No. 141 (Earl May); Midget Hybrid (Parks).
Cucumber:	Cherokee (Parks); Patio-Pik No. 366 (Earl May).
Eggplant:	Morden Midget (Parks); Early Beauty Hybrid (Burpee).
Lettuce:	Tom Thumb (Burpee, Parks); Midget No. 414 (Earl May).
Summer Squash:	St. Pat Scallop (Burpee); Hybrid Zucchini (Burpee).
Tomatoes:	Pixie Hybrid (Burpee); Tiny Tim (Burpee, Earl May, Parks); Pretty Patio (Earl May).
Watermelon:	New Hampshire Midget (Burpee, Earl May); Lollipop (Parks); Little Midget (Parks); Sugar Baby (Parks, Burpee, Earl May).

Think mini but think many.

119

Five-Foot Farm No. 5

FARMER McGREGOR'S—A TYPICAL SALAD
AND VEGETABLE GARDEN

Sketched below is a typical garden which can be contained in five feet and which should produce enough vegetables for at least two people for the best part of the summer. Of course, you don't have to follow this pattern—you can work out your own. Wherever you plant your tomatoes, though, plant marigolds nearby. They exude a chemical from their roots that keeps nematodes (tiny wormlike pests which attack roots) from damaging tomato and pepper plants.

The Cucumber Monster

To your salad garden you might also be able to tuck in a cucumber. Children enjoy watching this plant grow to see how the baby cucumber pushes out right from behind the blossom, with the flower petals still attached to the front end of the young fruit.

Your children can either train their cucumber vine to a fence or wall trellis, or let it run along the ground. With the latter, however, the children must watch to see that the vine does not run all over the other crops. This they will like. They will enjoy tending a rampant cucumber, vigilant to see that it keeps its place while threading through the garden. A pinch-back when the vine threatens to overrun the radishes, a turning-and-staking when tendrils are reaching out to clutch a green pepper plant, will have your children on their toes, keeping harmony in the garden.

Assign a child as a lookout to defend the other plants from the approach of the Cucumber Monster, and you will have a staunch guardian of the garden all through the summer.

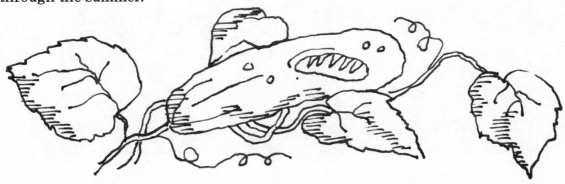

Five-Foot Farm No. 6

A WHATZIT GARDEN

Even if your family already boasts a young gardener or part-time farmer, there are probably many crops that he still has not had the opportunity to grow. (No farmer ever gets around to planting *everything* he would like to.) So if you can manage an additional little plot, how about devoting it to those let's-see-what-they-look-like types? Your choice will be restricted somewhat, of course, by the climate where you live. The long, warm growing season necessary for peanuts, for example, will rule out peanuts as an outdoor crop in Michigan.

Still, there are some "whatzit" crops for every clime. Here are a few for your consideration; you can make a patch of just one whatzit or try two or three different things.

Asparagus: You can order roots through seed-house catalogs. The biggest problem here is that the smallest amount offered is usually 50 roots—way too many for a small spot and a whatzit motive. But maybe you can divide up with others. A few garden centers are now beginning to offer asparagus roots in smaller quantities— 6 to a package. Asparagus roots can even be grown in a large flowerpot, and the roots have an octopuslike appearance that makes them fun for children to plant.

Brussel sprouts: You'd never guess how these grow—try one and see.

Eggplant: For sheer beauty, no other vegetable comes close. See page 124.

Corn: Remember to plant at least 4 rows to assure good pollination. See page 116.

Lima beans: Space these between the corn plants.

Peanuts: See page 115.

Okra: You'll have an exotic hibiscuslike flower in the morning, and by nightfall the beginnings of the okra pod under the wilted blossom.

Rhubarb: Order roots from a seed catalog; they can also now be found in some garden shops. These are sold in quantities as small as 3 roots, or even by the root. They make lovely plants that would grace any flower bed.

Five-Foot Farm No. 7

THE NIGHTSHADES—TOMATO, PEPPER AND EGGPLANT

The tomato, pepper and eggplant are all members of the nightshade family, but they are not at all like their sinister relative the deadly nightshade *(Solanum nigrum)*. The tomato's reputation, however, was not so good itself for a long time, and early settlers in this country believed they were poisonous. The eggplant, too, has emerged from a background of superstition, for it was once believed that a mere bite of it would make you insane.

These three vegetables are satisfying plants for children to grow. They are easy to care for and grow quickly, and the development and ripening of the fruit are almost measurable day by day. They are dependable plants, with low failure rates and few demands (mainly warm temperatures, sun and water). And they more than pay their way in the quality and quantity of fruit produced.

Plants of each of these vegetables can be purchased in the spring from local garden supply houses. Each one is also easily grown from seed, and all can be started indoors at the same time—about 8 weeks before it's time to plant outside. Study your seed catalog and decide which variety of each vegetable to order. One seed catalog offers 32 different varieties of tomatoes! Some have been developed for very large fruits, some for very small, some for a shorter season, some for low acid content, and so on.

Here's the fun of reading the seed catalog and the description of each variety. Oh, the choices you must make—which will it be? Sometimes, though, you will recognize *your* variety right away as having just the characteristics you are looking for.

After your seeds arrive, plant them as described in Getting Started (pages 53-59). When the young plants reach a height of 10 to 12 inches, you can move them to "second-stage" containers. Make these out of 2-pound coffee cans that come with plastic lids. Cut both metal ends from each can with a can opener, leaving an open-ended metal cylinder. Then put the plastic lid on the bottom of

the can. Now put in a couple of inches of gravel and soil, add one plant, and then fill the rest of the can with regular garden soil, covering the stalk of the tomato right up to the top of the can. Here the plants can be "held" until the outdoor weather settles to dependably warm.

When setting out, remove the plastic cover from the bottom, and sink the can into the ground along with the plant, leaving only an inch or so of the rim above ground. This provides excellent protection from the tomato's and pepper's arch enemy, the cutworm.

When preparing for planting outdoors, let the children dig a big planting hole, as big as a bushel basket. Then fill in most of it with your mulch (see page 64) or peat moss (bought at any garden store). Plants will also benefit greatly if cow manure is added before the plant goes into the ground. (In rural areas and some suburban communities, cow manure is added by the shovelful; in urban settings, cow manure comes in boxes from the hardware store or garden center!)

No additional fertilizer will be needed until the fruits begin to form. You can then topdress the plants with more manure, spread on the surface of the soil around each plant.

IN BASKETS, BARRELS, BAGS

Tomatoes in a Basket

Perhaps you have read through the Five-Foot Farms and would like to try some of them, but you live in a high-rise apartment, and do not have access to even five feet of earth. Brace up! There are ways for you to participate in gardening projects even if you have only a balcony or a sunny windowsill.

For example, you can *hang* your garden. And remember, baskets can be hung low as well as high, so you might be able to fit in as many as three baskets in your one sunny spot!

There are many hanging baskets on the market in a variety of shapes and sizes and colors. Some are of a molded polyethylene which offers the advantages of strength combined with light weight. A new circular design is available that will fit around a lamppost or dress up a balcony post.

Of course, a lot of fun can be had in looking for the offbeat hanging container. Almost anything that will contain a plant can be used as a hanging basket if it is not *too* heavy. You may have seen several "baskets" and just not recognized them!

An old colander from the kitchen or a new one from the dime store.

A dishpan or saucepan with a handle on each side. Punch several holes in the bottom for drainage.

A fish basket.

A wire salad-greens washer.

Drip-getters, to catch the water that drains through, will not be necessary if you line your baskets with sphagnum moss as described below, and water the plants carefully.

To prepare the baskets for planting, you will need a package of long-fibered sphagnum moss (available at garden supply houses and most dime stores). You will need about ¼ pound per 12-inch-diameter basket at a cost of about $1. Place the moss in a deep container to soak up water; it will take several hours for the

127

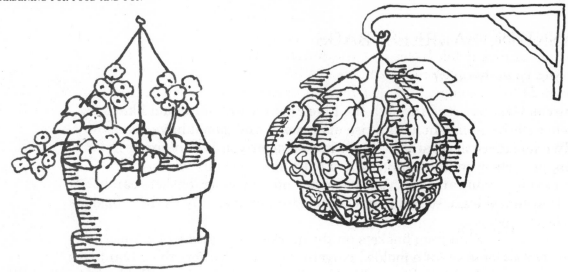

moss to become completely saturated. Then squeeze out the excess water and line the bottom and sides of your hanging container with a good thickness of the sphagnum moss—at least 1 inch for the sides and 2 inches for the bottom. Then add the soil. A mixture of about one third soil and two thirds vermiculite will provide enough nutrients for the plants and will be lightweight, too. Now you are ready to plant.

Vegetables that will work in hanging baskets include midget varieties of tomatoes and cucumbers, as well as leaf lettuce, radishes, and beets.

Some flowers are petunias, fuchsias, begonias, ferns (great!), Swedish ivy, and nasturtiums.

Lots of herbs, and peanuts, too, can be grown.

Watering hanging baskets requires some special techniques, none of them difficult. You can hang a drip-getter just below your hanging basket and then water the basket as you would any house plant. Or you can lower the baskets into a larger water-filled container and let them soak up water, drain and then rehang. Or you can—children like this method best—just toss several ice cubes up into the basket. The plant will be given a leisurely drink as the cubes melt.

128

Strawberries in a Barrel

You don't have to have a large area for a strawberry patch, either. You can grow these luscious treats "in the round."

Strawberry planter jars are available in garden stores. They look like large vases with holes or "pockets" around the sides. You can use such a jar for your strawberry patch, although they will provide for only a smallish crop.

You can make a better container yourself if you have an old barrel or a nail keg. Barrels are best sought in out-of-the way country stores. In city and suburb they can be awfully expensive. Sometimes kegs can be begged from highway crews, who receive hardware in them. They can also be bought at lumber stores for $3 to $5. After you find your barrel or keg, you will need to drill 1-inch-diameter holes about 8 inches apart, in staggered rows, around the outside of it. (If you don't have access to a drill, ask to have this done at the lumber store. They'll likely be willing to do the job for you and for only a small charge.) Place the barrel in what will be its permanent spot, for after it is filled with dirt and planted, it will be too heavy for you to move.

Place about a 2-inch layer of coarse gravel in the bottom of the barrel for drainage. Now take a mailing tube or a hollow pipe or roll up a piece of fairly stiff plastic into a 2-inch cylinder to stand in the middle of the barrel. Fill the tube with gravel and keep it in place while you begin filling the barrel with the richest soil you have. Tuck the strawberry plants (from the outside in, roots first) into each hole as the soil level reaches it. Water as you go along to settle the soil so that the whole thing won't slump in later on. Continue until the barrel is filled and then space a few more plants on top. You must be careful to place the "crown" of the strawberry plant (the point which divides the top from the roots) at ground level in order for the plants to grow. Now you can remove the cylinder from the center. The gravel core that remains will help water drain down through the barrel and out to the plants.

Plants can be purchased from garden supply stores or ordered from seed houses. For a better crop, choose the June-bearing varieties rather than the

129

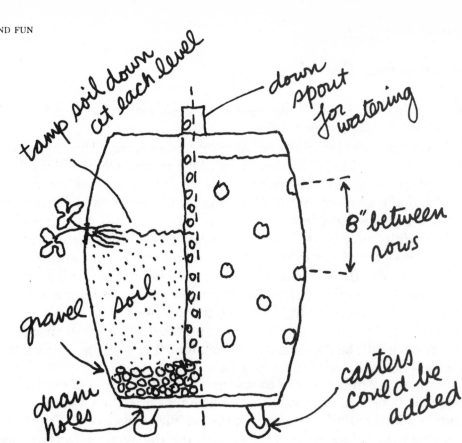

everbearing varieties. If you plant your strawberries very early in the spring, your plants will begin to bloom in May. You will get small berries the first year, so usually it is better to pick off the blossoms as they appear and not let your plants have berries the first year. (Well, pick off *almost* all the blooms. Small or not, it's worth having at least a *few* berries to taste the first year.) But the next year! Just wait! You will have large delicious berries. Your strawberry plants can withstand mild winter temperatures, but they should be protected with some kind of covering—a heavy mulch or a plastic cover during periods of very cold temperatures.

130

Potatoes in a Bag

Now for potatoes. Try growing your crop in a plastic bag filled with soil. Here's how to grow a bag of potatoes.

Cut a couple of white potatoes into pieces so that each piece has two or three eyes (buds). This is the same kind of "seed" farmers use to plant their potato crop.

Use a sturdy plastic trash-can liner for your bag. A 17-inch-wide by 18-inch-high bag will become a 10-inch-round by 8-inch-high one by the time it is prepared for planting. A pretty good size.

First fold the bag over at the top a couple of times to make a 2- to 3-inch cuff so that the bag will stay open neatly at the top. You will also need a large enough "saucer" of some sort to catch the drainage if the bag is to be kept indoors. An old kitchen tray, the top of a potato-chip can or a shallow roasting pan will work.

Put a good layer of gravel in the bottom of the bag—a half inch or so—and then punch a few holes in the bottom and bottom edge of the bag for drainage.

Now add soil up to within 3 inches of the top, and arrange the potato pieces around in the bag, about 4 inches apart.

Cover with more soil—a couple of inches—then water and put in a sunny place.

If you plant your potatoes about the end of March (or April in a northern climate), then when the days are warm enough you can put the bag out on the balcony or patio, where it will get the most sun possible. Before fall arrives you will have grown yourself a sack of potatoes!

IN THE KITCHEN AFTER THE HARVEST

You are only halfway along to growing green when you tend your own garden; the other half is in knowing how to handle the produce from it.

In growing vegetables, it's fun to let some of them go the limit. Actually no good gardener can resist it—seeing how big the squash will grow (huge), how fat the radish will be (enormous), how long the cucumber (really long).

For best *eating,* though, try to harvest your crops before they get too big (old). You'll surely want to taste squash that is still tiny and tender; the same for green peas, radishes, all your crops. Enjoy showing off the size and shapes of the vegetables you produce; but don't forget to enjoy the *taste* of them, too. You will learn a great deal about all the vegetables you grow when you have a chance to sample them at various stages, from young to old.

The easiest way to eat them, of course, is right on the spot. If you have never eaten raw vegetables straight from the garden, you will be surprised to find them very good munching, indeed.

As for cooking, you need remember one main thing: the two worst enemies of fresh vegetables are water and heat.

If your vegetables need to be washed before cooking, make it a quick rinse. No soaking. When cooking, use as little water as possible. A half a cup is plenty in an average-size saucepan. Have the water boiling before the vegetables go in. Use a rack if you have one, put on a tight-fitting lid, and steam the vegetables. Six to eight minutes should do for most vegetables—less for some.

You can also stir-fry vegetables the way the Chinese do, if not in a wok then in a skillet, using no water at all. Cut the vegetables in small pieces, heat just a bit of oil and stir-fry the vegetables fast—till they're just tender but still crisp. *Not* soft and soggy. *Never!* Soft and soggy vegetables are probably why some kids don't like vegetables in the first place. You have a whole new tasting world ahead of you when you can cook vegetables you have grown yourself, and cook them right.

Another couple of things about harvesting. No matter how small the crop, be certain that it winds up as a special part of an eating event, say, dinner, or as a special nibble during the day. You may have only a few peas or green beans from the one container plant the young gardener insisted on having in his room. Well, these could make a one-for-you, one-for-me, on-the-spot snack. Or they could go into a salad to add a special, fresh-from-the-garden crunch to it. Or freeze the few odd peas or beans as they come along till you have enough for a serving for each family member or at least a serving for the gardener. (Before freezing them, blanch by

133

popping them into hot water, then cold.)

Four or five radishes—the *total* radish harvest from a five-year-old's five-foot garden—could be delicious when thin-sliced on buttered bread for an afternoon sandwich; or why not radish roses to garnish either a main dish or individual salads?

At the other extreme are the bumper crops that need special attention, too. *Don't* let any of your lovely vegetables stay on the vine growing old simply because you have more than you can eat or you have wearied of eating fresh squash or fresh cucumbers or such. The latter circumstances may be hard to imagine ever happening, and they won't if you do any one of a number of things, the most obvious being to share with those who do not have access to a garden. Or set up a fresh vegetable stand where young farmers can sell their excess produce. And keep an eye out for new recipes and new ways to combine your crops in new dishes. No better time for the young gardener to discover the pleasure that comes from preparing and serving good food than when it is food he has grown himself.

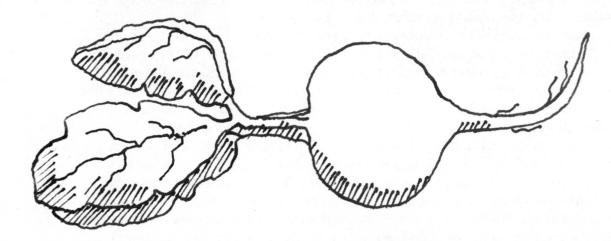

BIG-BANG GARDENING

Lots of gardening activities can be pursued for the sheer fun of it—to come up with something different or simply to see what will happen. Children never fail to get a big bang out of the offbeat or unusual gardening adventure. Here are a few ideas to get you started. You will think of others that suit your own interests and family "personality."

Cucumbers in a Bottle

You've heard of cucumbers in a flowerpot? They are as easy to grow in containers as are other vegetables such as tomatoes, green peppers and eggplant.

But what about cucumbers in a bottle? Kids are always fascinated with the ships, fully rigged and sails set, that are enclosed inside a narrow-necked bottle. Parents are equally intrigued at first sight of a special type of brandy which contains within its narrow-necked bottle a beautiful full-grown pear.

How the ship winds up in the bottle belongs in another book. As for the pear, it is placed inside the bottle while the fruit is still on the tree and small enough to slip through the neck. The bottle is then fastened securely to the branch of the tree, and the pear grows to full size inside its glass house. The pear is harvested right along with the bottle, and the brandy is added later. *Voila!* Pear brandy.

You can borrow this technique from the brandy maker to grow a cucumber in a bottle! Or a squash. Select a clear glass bottle. The type that salad oil comes in is a good choice because it has a small opening but a short neck. When the cucumber fruit has set on the vine and is about 2 inches long, but still smaller in diameter than the bottle opening, slip the fruit inside the bottle. Be careful not to break, bruise or otherwise damage the stem end or the vine. A small part of it will need to poke into the bottle, too, which is why a short-necked bottle, such as the salad-oil type, works best.

Place the bottle on the ground, under the sheltering leaves of the vine. Keep a watch on it while the cucumber grows so that the bottle and the fruit inside are not exposed to direct sun all day. Cucumbers like to nestle in under the leaves of the vine, and you may have to shift your bottle gently every now and then so that it remains sheltered. Let your cucumber grow as big as you like inside the bottle. If it is a squash you are growing, watch it almost day by day, for it grows both big and fast and will fill the jar before you know it.

You will want to show off your new gardening wonder to as many people as

136

you can, as fast as you can, because the cucumber obviously will not last long in its glass house—a couple of weeks at most under refrigeration. Before its time runs out, reach in the jar with a long, thin sharp knife and cut the cucumber in lengthwise strips that can then be slipped out. You won't likely be able to make precision cuts, and the resulting pieces will be tattered perhaps, but they will make good eating just the same.

And plan to eat it. Otherwise you will find it depressing to see your lovely bottle vegetable go soft, shrivel and generally turn into a mess.

Cress Quick

Plan to place your dish of cress on the breakfast table or on a shady kitchen windowsill. Keep a small pair of scissors there, and the children can snip off enough cress in the morning to garnish their scrambled eggs or omelet, to sprinkle on top of a bowl of soup or to tuck into a sandwich.

There are several ways to grow cress at table side. Choose a shallow bowl or a saucer. (Or one child might be delighted to have a garden growing in the flat bed of a small plastic toy truck; another might choose a toy pie pan).

Crumple up a paper tissue or two, moisten and put into the container. Moisten another tissue and lay it flat across the top of the others. Now sprinkle the cress seeds on top. Within the next day or two, the children can see that the seeds have split and the tiny cress sprouts are beginning to emerge. Keep the tissues always moist by adding a small amount of water to the edge of the tissues, so as not to disturb the tiny seedlings, and within a couple of weeks the cress will be far enough along to harvest—a snip here, a snip there. If you've got a picky eater, a bit of cress may just turn the trick. It's been known to happen.

Also, an elegant tea party—small bread-butter-and-cress sandwiches (and for a really elegant one, very, very thin slices of cucumber, too) along with a cup of hot tea—is lots of fun for a small person just home from school with a friend.

Another method of planting cress that children will enjoy is done on top of a sponge. Buy a flat-type sponge and let the children cut their initials or a design out of it. Put it in a container; a metal soap dish with a separate drain tray works perfectly. Keep the sponge moist and the seeds will sprout to form a green circle or square or letter.

If you want a longer-lasting, taller, bigger crop of cress, then plant the seeds in soil. (See The ABC's of Gardening, page 53 .) With moist soil, you will be clipping and munching for weeks because you can sprinkle on new seed as you harvest your crop. Mustard seed grows equally well, making a larger plant than cress—and also tastes just as good snipped and sprinkled over various dishes.

Pumpkin Derby

Why not sponsor a pumpkin derby?

Purchase from the garden-supply house or order from the seed catalog Big Max pumpkin seeds. Then in early summer give three or four pumpkin seeds and complete instructions on how to grow them (copied from the seed package) to each participant.

Each child is to plant his own seeds and take care of the plants. Set a date for the harvest time. For Big Max variety, it should be 120 days after planting.

Remind growers that to get the largest possible pumpkin, they should pick off all but two or three of the pumpkins as they reach softball size. To get a jump on the competition, after the pumpkins reach basketball size, select one for "force feeding." Make a lengthwise slit in the stem and insert a long cloth wick (a length cut from an old towel will do). Place the other end of the wick in a plastic jug of water. Keep the jug sheltered from the hot sun by placing it under the plant's leaves. This gives the pumpkin a direct pipeline to the water—and pumpkins need lots of that.

Contestants may also scrape their name or initials on the pumpkins with a dull knife, working carefully and penetrating just the outer skin. The writing will grow larger along with the pumpkin.

The date for the pumpkin judging, of course, is also the date for a wonderful

harvest or Halloween party, with the main event the pumpkin judging. The pumpkins can be judged for girth (measurement around the fattest part); for weight; for deepest color; and anything else you can think of that might distinguish one pumpkin from another. Keep thinking until everyone wins in *some* category.

Of course, jack-o'-lanterns and toasted pumpkin seeds are in the offing, too. For the latter, sort the seeds out from the pulp. This will be gooey and sticky going and therefore loads of icky fun for the kids. Rinse the seeds thoroughly through a colander. Blot dry in toweling. Spread out in a shallow, greased pan and put in a 300-degree oven for a few minutes, watching them to see that they don't burn and turning them with a spatula. Salt lightly and eat while they're warm.

Bean Sprouts Fast

Mung beans are perhaps the fastest seed-to-table crop there is. Would you believe five days? Such fast growth and the prospect of cooking and eating the crop make bean sprouts an exciting project for youngsters.

Mung beans are available in many large groceries and in most oriental food shops—or they can be ordered from a seed house. These beans used to be imported from Asia, but now they are increasingly grown in the United States. About half a cup of beans will be plenty for one "planting"—enough to add to at least two dishes.

Wash the beans well, picking them over as you would for cooking, and then soak them overnight in cold water. The beans will swell to about three times their original size.

Drain and place the beans in an ordinary clay flowerpot—8 to 10 inches in diameter—either new or scrubbed thoroughly clean, with the drain hole covered loosely with a few clean rocks or a piece of nylon net. Cover the beans with a clean damp cloth and put in a dark place, such as underneath the kitchen sink or in a kitchen cabinet. If the beans are exposed to daylight or even electric lights during these few days, the sprouts will be a slightly pink or green color—not the white, which is considered more attractive in foods.

Let the children check the beans twice a day. They can put the pot in the sink and gently run water through it, rinsing the beans and leaving the cloth damp before putting the pot back in the dark.

(You can also use a screw-top jar instead of a flowerpot if you punch a lot of holes in the lid so that the water can be drained off. Choose a wide-mouthed jar with a dark color to it—this protects the sprouts from light. Some kinds of applesauce are packed in an amber or brown glass that works very well. Otherwise, handle the same as described above.)

The sprouts should be ready to eat in five days and will reach optimum size in seven days. After harvesting, they will keep for two or three more days in the refrigerator if stored in a closed plastic bag.

These nutritious, delicious little packages of food can be used in lots of different recipes or simply nibbled raw as a snack. Here are a couple of easy dishes that children enjoy making.

FRIED CHINESE VEGETABLES

Cut into bite-size pieces any or all of the following: celery, carrots, onion, broccoli, green pepper, radishes. (Actually, your youngster can take a look in the vegetable crisper on any given day and pick out the two or three vegetables he thinks will taste and look good together.)

Into a hot fry pan pour 2 tablespoons of salad oil. Add the vegetables. Stir-fry till tender but still crisp. (See In the Kitchen After the Harvest, page 132.) Just before the vegetables are done, add a handful of bean sprouts and cook just long enough to heat them up. Serve at once. Quick, good eating and good for you!

RAI-SUN-SPROUT BALLS

Chop up fine 1 cup of sprouts, 1 cup of raisins, ½ cup of shelled sunflower seeds. Mix together well and put in the refrigerator to chill. Form into small balls and roll in either coconut or the crunchy kind of cereal.

Great Gourd Fun

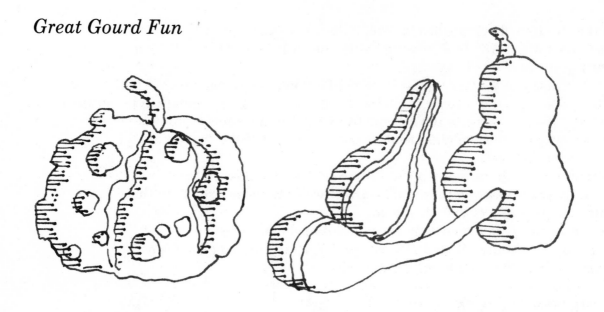

Gourds are easily grown and can be enjoyed by every member of the family. The seeds can be ordered according to the size of fruit desired and are generally divided into large and small types. Both types provide hundreds of gourds varying in shape, texture and color. This makes for the most fun part of growing gourds— finding out what your fruit looks like and what use each shape will inspire you to make of it. You can make birdhouses, dippers, candleholders, centerpieces, bowls, pitchers, funnels and decorations—and any other things you can think of. Some varieties of gourds have been named according to the use most frequently made of them—and so from your seed catalog you can order dipper gourds (sometimes known as calabash gourds), birdhouse gourds, spoon gourds and others.

Ideally, gourd seeds are planted 3 to 5 seeds to a "hill," or mound of soil. They can be sown outside after the danger of frost has passed; or you can start seeds indoors in late February or early March. Use the little peat pots and follow planting directions on the package. (See the basics in The ABC's of Gardening, page 53.)

The seeds should germinate within a week—even sooner if you soak them overnight before planting. After the seedlings have reached a height of 2 to 3 inches, and when all the seeds have germinated, then with manicure scissors reach in and snip off at the ground line all but the hardiest of the seedlings. This may seem a heartless way to treat tiny plants, but if you try to transplant the other seedlings, you will probably damage the root systems of all of them in the process. And there won't be enough room, food or water to support more than one plant. So all but one should go.

Place the seedling in the sunniest window you have. As soon as the roots begin to grow through the mesh covering of the peat pot, it is time to transplant outside if the weather is dependably warm by then. If not, or if you live in an apartment, a 3-pound coffee can or larger flowerpot will make a fine container. Use ordinary garden dirt, adding leaf mold, compost or dried manure (it comes packaged at garden stores). Place the container where it will get as much sun as possible.

The maturing plant does require some room to "run" in and some support by means of a trellis, balcony railing or fence. If you are an apartment dweller, you will probably want to limit your crop to one container, but that will still give you plenty of gourds to work with.

The vine will grow all summer, and as the various sizes and shapes of the gourds take form, your daily inspection will be enlivened by discovering the new ones—those that are "different from any we've already had."

Let the gourds remain on the vine until after frost. Then they should be picked or cut from the dry vines with a sharp knife, taking a short part of the stem along with them.

The smaller gourds will require no special treatment for preservation. They need only be air-dried, and they can be ornamental in the process. Simply arrange them in a bowl or basket. Or you can drill small holes in the ends of them and string them with a stout cord and hang them in your room or on the porch. After they are thoroughly dry—when you can hear the seeds rattling around inside—you can shellac them if you wish. Though this is not necessary for the gourds' preservation, it will help to keep their colors bright for a longer period of time.

The larger gourds need to be thoroughly dry before you cut them to make other articles. Check their dryness by shaking them. If the seeds rattle around inside, the gourds are dry enough to work with.

The dipper gourd is the type that served so many useful purposes in American farm homes as recently as fifty years ago. Hardly a country household that depended on a well for their water supply was without the services of a dipper gourd hanging nearby from which to sip the clear well water. You can duplicate the pioneers' dippers today, for the seeds of the dipper gourds are available from many seed companies. The gourds mature at various sizes but are of the same general shape: a long narrow top enlarging to a round ball shape at the bottom.

Use a sharp knife and very carefully slice off one side of the ball. Now you can remove all the seeds and fibers from inside the gourd. (Remember to save the seeds for the birds.) If you like, drill a small hole in the top of the neck and insert a string for hanging the dipper. Use it to drink from or just for decoration. Fun to keep in the bathroom for your own drinking cup.

Penguin gourds or goose gourds grow in shapes that bear a strong resemblance to these birds. After these gourds are thoroughly dry, the features of the bird can be painted on with acrylic paints or with enamel. They can then be mounted on bases for display. A plain piece of wood, given a coat of stain and varnish or just clear varnish, will make a good base. Glue your gourd bird in place.

The dishrag gourd looks like a super cucumber. A yard long is not uncommon. The main interest in this variety, though, lies in the inside fibers, which are so tough and durable that they make excellent sponges. In fact, if you have a sizable crop of dishrag gourds, you could make some spending money by selling the dishrag sponges. They are great for washing dishes and general household cleaning. Just one demonstration will get you a customer every time!

The birdhouse gourd has an elongated oval shape that birds find very suitable for nesting—especially the purple martins. And who wouldn't welcome this splendid bird to his yard. As with other gourds, pick the birdhouse gourd after frost, when it is completely ripe. Let it dry until the seeds rattle inside.

Then with a small-bladed saw or sharp knife cut a hole in the side of the gourd about halfway up from the bottom. The seeds will have to be shaken out through this hole. The size of the hole you make will determine to a large extent the future occupants of the house. For purple martins, make the hole 2 ⅛ inches in diameter. Below this hole, punch a smaller one about ¼ inch in diameter. Insert a round stick in this hole to provide a perch. Then in the neck of the gourd, drill or punch a small hole through which a cord can be strung in order to hang the gourd from a pole or tree. This is the very method the Indians used to attract purple martins to their villages.

Bean Olympics

You may often have seen a tuft of grass growing through a crack in the sidewalk. Or sometimes a plant growing out from a rocky wall. You may not have realized, though, that it is the sprouting seed that makes the sidewalk or wall crack and admit the tiny plant to sunlight. A seed has a great deal of explosive energy packed away in it.

You can get an idea of the force that a sprouting seed can exert from an experiment you can do at home or with your friends at school. The experiment can be conducted as a weight-lifting event to determine the maximum weight a typical bean seed can lift in its attempt to sprout!

You can use any type of bean for this activity; whatever you have on hand in the kitchen cupboard—navy beans, lima beans, pintos, etc. You will need 8 beans, 36 pennies, and about 50 toothpicks.

Soak the beans overnight. This will get them into condition to perform faster.

While they are soaking, prepare a seed bed, or flat, in any shallow dish or pan. A rectangular cake pan will do nicely. Line it with foil, first, if it happens to be a best and only, or if the owner has a thing about ever again using a kitchen utensil that may once have served in the line of gardening duty.

Put a layer of fine gravel or coarse sand about ¼ inch thick in the bottom to insure good drainage. Then fill the pan with potting soil, which will provide a smoother surface than garden dirt.

145

Space the 8 beans about 2 inches apart in the pan and press them firmly and evenly into the soil. Then place a penny directly over the first bean. Over the second bean place 2 pennies; over the third, 3 pennies; and so on until the eighth bean is planted with 8 pennies resting directly over it.

Now place toothpicks around the edges of the pennies to keep them fenced in as the beans sprout. Otherwise, the pennies will be tipped over and pushed aside.

You may be surprised at the results in a few days. Sometimes the contestant with several pennies is able to hoist them quicker than the contestant with only one!

Another Olympic event might be a weight-lifting contest among individual beans. Prepare the seed flat as described above, leveling the soil and spacing the beans about 2 inches apart. Then as each contestant is planted, place only one penny (on which you have taped a number) over each bean. Arrange toothpicks around the pennies as before, to hold them in place as the sprouts begin to emerge from the soil. The first bean to upend its coin would be declared the winner of the Bean Olympics. All contestants could be honored by being transplanted to a garden plot and given plenty of tender loving care. Perhaps some of *their* seeds will grow to compete in the next Bean Olympics.

A Fantastic Flower—The Amaryllis

Among the members of the flower world, the amaryllis is one of the most dramatic in performance and appearance. Its growth is so rapid it can be measured almost daily, and its huge, lilylike blooms provide enough impact to impress even the most blasé among us.

The amaryllis bulbs are on the expensive side—as much as $5 or so for one bulb. If you watch at discount houses and such, though, you will see them advertised for less sometimes. But buy the larger size rather than the small if it comes to a choice, since as long as you are going for a spectacular in the flower world, you might as well have the most spectacular. And if you take care of the bulb, you can have repeat performances from it year after year.

You can also try the more-from-one route with the amaryllis, too. (See Making More from One, page 69) When you repot it for the beginning of a new season, watch for little offset bulblets that the parent bulb produces. If you keep these growing, they will be blooming for you, too, in a couple of years, and you will be amaryllis-*rich*. You can also try harvesting and planting seeds for more bulbs. More on this later.

You can pot your bulb in a mixture of peat moss and vermiculite, or you can give it royal treatment by mixing up a potting concoction that contains one part dirt, one part sand, one part leaf mulch (see page 65), and a tablespoon of bone meal, good for all bulbs. Then water the whole thing with a manure "tea"—that's what it's called—which is water mixed with a bit of packaged manure fertilizer.

The amaryllis has a large bulb, and the container you use should have at least an inch to spare all around. Plant the bulb so that the top third of it is above ground.

Now put it in a warm place and give it only a *very little* water to get it growing. Once the leaves appear, the growth will be astonishing, and you will want to water it more to keep it going. The soil should be moist, but never soggy.

The plant will reach a height of 2 feet and be blooming magnificently within three to five weeks. Quite a performance!

When the amaryllis is in bloom, the six large stamens within each flower are loaded with bright yellow pollen. Children will find it interesting first to see the quantity of pollen produced—they need only touch the top of the stamen, and their fingers will be covered with thick yellow pollen. Then let them select one of the flowers for transferring the pollen to the pistil. Use a small watercolor brush, and simply dab it on the anther (the top of the stamen) to take up some of the pollen and transfer it onto the stigma (the sticky top of the pistil).

These various parts of the plant (the stamens and pistil) are large and easy to work with in the amaryllis. Later you will find yourself looking much more carefully at other flowers to see how these seed-making parts differ from flower to flower. The differences are great and extensive and as fascinating a part of nature as any could be. (And a good bit more complex than the story of the birds and bees

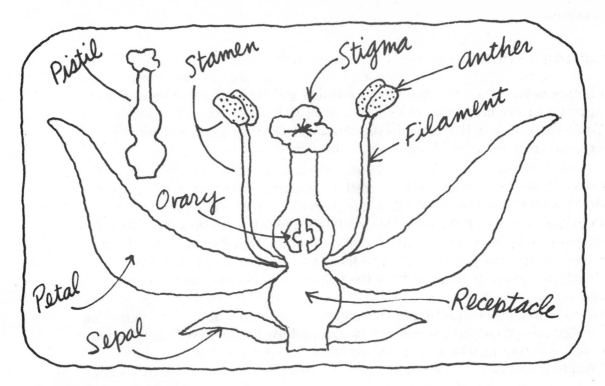

would lead us to believe.)

After the flowers fade, cut off all but the bloom you have pollinated and wait for the seed pod to form. Don't cut off the leaves—the bulb needs these to manufacture food for next year's blooms.

Keep feeding the plant regularly at least every two weeks. Within four weeks a fat, tricorn-shaped green seed pod will have formed on the flower stalk. Let it stay on the plant to ripen. When it opens, you will find the seeds! In thin, flat, black, ashlike layers. From these you can begin your "own" amaryllis.

The parent bulb can now be put outdoors for the summer, fed and watered regularly and brought back in before frost. Then cut off the leaves and let the plant rest for two to three months—no water, no food. Then you will want to pot it up again with a fresh beginning as described above (look for bulblets now), and it will be ready for another year's big-bang performance.

148

Onions and Petunias

A maybe-a-bit-kooky, but not crazy, birthday gift for the garden enthusiast who happens to have been born in February or March is a fat bunch of green onion slips. You'll find these in the seed houses and garden shops from the first days of February and on into March. And you will also find that these are a gift that never fails to delight.

The gift container can be varied—from the very simple to the elegant. Those pencil holders from juice cans that no child escapes making at some point in primary school turn out to be perfect containers for bunches of onion slips. The slips will keep several weeks—which is long enough for even an early February gift because onions are one of the first crops to be planted in early spring. For that last added touch, include a package of petunia seeds. (If you or your kids have never heard the song about the lonely little petunia in the onion patch, find someone who knows it and have him run through it for you.)

For some reason, grandfathers are crazy about this gift, so if your child has a February-March grandfather, put onions and petunias on his gift list. He will get a big bang out of them.

Puppet Planters

If grandfathers find onions and petunias a great gardening gift, grandmothers go a bit dotty over puppet planters presented by a young gardening relative.

The container for the puppet planter is the small plastic hand puppet often given away as advertising novelties by hamburger or pizza restaurants.

Fill the plastic puppet bag completely with potting soil, making sure the little arms are also filled. Now, with water from the tap running in a very fine stream, hold the soil-filled bag under the faucet until the soil is moistened throughout. It should be just damp rather than soggy.

Fasten the end of the bag securely with a rubber band or twistum. Puncture

149

about 6 holes around the bag about ½ inch up from the bottom to
allow water to soak in later on. Use a pencil to punch holes through the front
side of the puppet's hands.

Now for the planting. Poke seeds into the damp soil with the pencil point to a depth about twice the diameter of the seed. Citrus seeds are ideal. They are readily available from your breakfast orange or grapefruit, make lovely ornamental plants, and will not outgrow the puppet bag for quite a while.

Stand the puppet upright now in a small shallow container—a saucer, soup dish, margarine tub or little round foil pan.

You must watch closely for your seeds to germinate and make sure that they are aimed right so they grow through the holes you have provided for them (which you may have to enlarge to accommodate their growth). When the little seedlings are up and growing well, it's gift-giving time. You can be absolutely certain that Ronald McDonald, Shotgun Sam, or whoever the puppet person is, will find a ready welcome when he appears bearing two young shiny green plants in his outstretched hands.

Forcing Bulbs

Producing spring flowers from bulbs is one of the most beautiful experiences

150

of the season. But maybe you live in an apartment; or do not have a suitable place in your yard for bulbs; or are not certain you are going to be living in your present home when spring rolls around. You still can share the joys of growing these flowers with your children and of giving them as gifts.

Paper whites (narcissus) bulbs are the easiest for forcing into bloom, but other bulbs, including those of the hyacinth and tulip, can also be brought to indoor bloom. Buy good-quality bulbs when they first come on the market in the fall, choosing the biggest ones you can find. Eight to a dozen of them will be enough for a nice display.

Paper whites can be planted in soil in an ordinary clay pot, and they can also be grown in a shallow container of water, nestled into a bed of pebbles or marbles.

If you use soil, which will provide more food for the bulbs' roots than water will, you will need a large flowerpot from 8 to 10 inches in diameter at the top. Place a piece of gravel or broken pot (every gardener has to have pieces of broken clay pots about—the beginner will just have to break one in order to get started) over the drainage hole and fill the pot about halfway with the soil—the richest you have. If you have compost, use it.

Now comes fun for the child, because he gets to place the bulbs around on top of the soil—close together but not touching one another. Then he can cover them all up with soil, firming gently around each bulb with his fingers and leaving just the tips of the bulbs showing, like noses sticking up out from under the covers. The exposed tips should be just below the top rim of the pot.

Now put the whole pot in the kitchen sink to soak up water from the bottom until the surface of the soil appears damp. The pot is then ready to "go off to bed" and your youngster can pick out a cool, dark place to put his soon-to-be spring flowers. A storage room or a seldom-opened closet will do.

Actually the bulbs will not be sleeping during this time; they will be busy forming root systems. Let your child peek in on the bulbs after about two weeks. The top of the bulbs should be beginning to grow by now, showing a pale yellow color. After this top growth is about 2 inches high, he can take the pot out of the closet and bring it into the light, but *not* hot, direct sunlight. Now the leaves and stems will really take off growing, turning a good green color, and flower buds will soon form.

Cool temperatures are preferable if you can manage it—perhaps in an entryway. Within a few more days, the buds will open to reward your patience with lovely blooms and a fantastic fragrance.

For forcing the paper whites in water (and children like this way, too), choose a large shallow bowl about 2 inches deep and fill it about halfway with pebbles, marbles or whatever drainage material you have. Snuggle the bulbs down into the pebbles, close to each other but not touching. Now put more pebbles in, covering the bulbs up to around their shoulders. Add water enough to just cover the pebbles.

For tulips and hyacinths, the root-forming period is much longer than for paper whites—at least twelve weeks. And during this time the bulbs must have cold temperatures. They can be kept outside on a protected part of the balcony, the pot wrapped with newspaper and plastic to keep the bulbs cold but not frozen; otherwise in a cool garage or storage area where temperatures do not exceed 40 degrees F. (The refrigerator would do if the proprietor of the house were willing to give up refrigerator space for three months, which is highly unlikely.) If you have a yard, the entire pot can simply be buried in the ground.

During this root-forming period the pot should be kept moist. The bulbs can be checked after about twelve weeks to see if top growth has started. (Your child will check them much earlier than that no doubt, but will probably not see any action until about that time.) When growth does start, the pots can be brought in and introduced to warmer temperatures. The blooms will last longer indoors if your room temperature is somewhat on the cool side. Water the bulbs whenever the surface soil feels dry. (Get in the habit of asking the children to check the soil to see if the plants need water and they'll be old pros at this important part of gardening within a very short time.)

Living Christmas Trees

Children—even from toddler stage—love having their "own" Christmas tree, one they can keep in their special place and decorate and undecorate as much as they wish, and any way they wish. So why not make their small tree a living one, and make it one that can grow up indoors right along with them? (Many families have already discovered the pleasure and advantages of making the *family* Christmas tree a living one and planting it outdoors after the holidays are over.)

Nothing will suit so well for an indoor Christmas tree as a Norfolk Island pine. These lovely, graceful plants can be purchased when they are only inches high, and can be found (not all the time, so keep an eye out for them) in discount, supermarket and dime stores as well as elegant nurseries. In fact, the small size is more likely to be found in the dime stores and such. They're inexpensive at that point and are a real bargain.

The pyramidal shape of the pine means that your youngster will have no trouble at all relating to this "house plant" as a Christmas tree, too. When he is old enough to manage them, a string of tiny sparkle lights as well as miniature ornaments he can collect or make himself will provide all the glitter he wants.

As the years go by, your investment in the tree grows, too. The toddler who starts out with a tiny tree costing under $1 will find himself as a teenager with a plant worth as much as $30 to $40. And priceless for you both as far as memories go.

BRANCHING OUT—INDOORS

When the last days of February roll around, youngsters and parents alike are suddenly weary of winter; and the longing for spring, and the renewal we know it will bring, is stirring in our minds and bodies. That's the time to hurry spring along —at least indoors. Almost nothing could be easier and more showy than forcing the branches of flowering shrubs and trees into indoor bloom. Forsythia, japonica, mock orange, honeysuckle (fantastic fragrance) and fruit-tree branches are suitable.

It is best to collect the branches on a day when the temperature is above freezing. Prune off fairly long (18 inches to 2 feet) branches—long enough to have several buds which will make a good show of color. Place inside a tall vase or planter; add enough water to cover the stem about one third of the depth of the container. Place where the branches will receive some sunlight every day.

The whole family will delight in watching the buds swell as the branches begin to believe that warmer weather has finally arrived. (In this case, it *is* nice to fool Mother Nature.) The buds will swell to bursting and then your waiting will be rewarded with a showy display and fragrance, guaranteed to brighten the home and lift you right out of the slumps. Add water as needed to maintain the third-full level and don't place near direct heat.

As for hammering the stems before placing in water, some scientists believe it does more harm than good because the pounding destroys a lot of tiny cells that should pass water up the stem to the buds. However, such information will not likely ever deter those green people who firmly believe that the pounding helps.

Since kids like to pound things, let them give the branch ends a few whacks, even in the face of scientific evidence to the contrary. As a matter of fact, let them play scientist themselves. They can give half of the branches a pounding, and the other half not. Tag one half or the other with small colored twistums. Put both groups in the same arrangement. Let the children keep close watch from day to day to see if they can detect any difference in budding, length of freshness, and bud and blossom drop from the branches.

5 Gardening Is Where You Find It

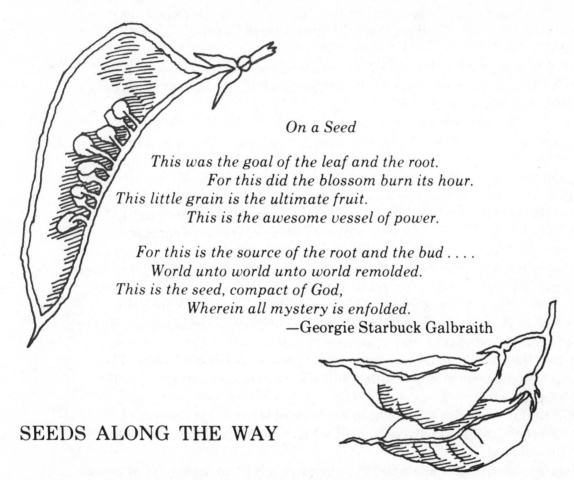

On a Seed

This was the goal of the leaf and the root.
     For this did the blossom burn its hour.
This little grain is the ultimate fruit.
     This is the awesome vessel of power.

For this is the source of the root and the bud . . . .
     World unto world unto world remolded.
This is the seed, compact of God,
     Wherein all mystery is enfolded.
          —Georgie Starbuck Galbraith

SEEDS ALONG THE WAY

The seeds that are the most fun to grow don't come in packets and aren't sold at the store. These are the seeds you find—anywhere. In the maple tree's helicopter, the pine tree's cone, the dogwood berry, the sycamore ball, the acorn of the mighty oak.

And there are more. You'll get a "Hey, that's a neat idea" if you suggest planting the fluff from a dandelion gone to seed. Children may not know, or care, that dandelions are "weeds" and that nobody grows them. A seed is a seed, so why not?

You may be surprised to discover that the seeds you find can present a real gardening challenge. Seeds that don't look complicated at all may not be as easy to germinate as you might think.

Partly that's because we are accustomed to flower and vegetable seeds that germinate soon after they are planted. They have been selected and bred to do their best for us.

But when we are dealing with seeds we find along the way, we may have an entirely different proposition on our hands.

Some of the seeds you find may require nothing more than water, light, warmth and a little bit of time, and they will send their new shoots right up through the soil. But others can be much more demanding.

Some seeds have built-in needs—"blocks," the scientists call them. Until these blocks are satisfied, the seed will not germinate. Blocks include a hard seed coat that keeps out moisture and/or oxygen. The seed will not germinate until this seed coat is softened, or dissolved, or scratched or rubbed off. Other seeds need to be kept cold and wet for a period of time (weeks or months), just as if it were winter for them, before they will sprout. And some seeds even have double blocks. They must be chilled, then warmed, then chilled and warmed again before they will sprout and keep growing.

You will find it great fun to see which seeds need what to get them to germinate, and there will be great excitement when you finally crack the code of a very stubborn seed.

Consider apple seeds, for example. They require a cold, moist period of two to three months. *But,* after you plant the seeds, if the temperature goes much above 75 degrees, more like hot summer weather than springtime, the seeds will revert to their blocked condition rather than sprout. This is called double dormancy.

And there is still more mystery to the apple seed. For you may find that the

156

seeds of an apple will germinate a few weeks after planting them without any special treatment at all. Actually, though, the seeds may have been getting their required cold period all the time they were inside the apple—it was chilled after picking, and kept cold during its shipment to and stay in the supermarket and while in your refrigerator before you took it out to eat!

So seeds can be a puzzle. Just wait till you try the lowly dandelion. You may get it to germinate easily enough (you will have to wait a few weeks perhaps), but can you keep it growing? You will have a new respect for the inner workings of this little plant which seems to have no trouble at all sprouting and growing relentlessly wherever people don't want it. Well, it can be just as stubborn in reverse, not growing when you want it to. Try it yourself and see!

Here are a few hints to help you grow the seeds you find along the way. First of all, it's a good idea to gather several of the seeds, so that if they don't germinate when planted under one set of circumstances, you will have others to plant in different ways to see if you can discover what it takes to wake them up. You can plant a few as described in Getting Started (pages 53-61), and if they don't germinate, then you can try other methods such as those described below.

To store the extra seeds until you are ready to plant them, put them in a tight container and keep them in a cool, dark place—the refrigerator is fine if you put them in a spot furthest away from the ice unit.

- Most tree seeds you find in the fall will germinate in the spring if planted when you find them. If you do not have a place to plant them outdoors, you can substitute for winter conditions by a process called "stratifying": moisten a small amount of peat moss and sand mixed together along with the seeds; put in a plastic bag and store in the refrigerator till spring (at least four months).

- Tree seeds you find in the spring can be hurried along or improved in germination by stratifying for two to three months.

- Some seeds need to be scarified—their seed coats scratched—to hasten germination. Try scratching the surface of the seed with a nail file, rubbing

157

gently till you have just broken through the hard outer coat so that moisture can enter.

● Occasionally you may come across a seed that takes a long, long time to germinate. The dogwood berry, for example, may hold out for as long as from fall to the following second spring. Obviously, then, gardening with seeds you find along the way can call for a good deal of patience. However, the rewards are great. The longer the wait, the more memorable the day when you spot a new seedling poking up through its covering.

● Some kinds of seeds that usually require the cold, moist treatment (stratifying) to get them to germinate include those from most alders, most ashes, bald cypresses, beeches, most birches, most buckeyes, cherries, American chestnuts, firs, hackberries, hemlocks, hickories, junipers, most larches, most maples, mulberries, black oaks, some pines (especially the white pines), plums, sassafras, some spruces, sweetgums, sycamores, tupelos, walnuts, white cedars and yellow poplars.

● Among the species that benefit from softening of the seed coat are the Kentucky coffee tree, honey locust and black locust.

● Seeds that may require a combination of seed coat softening and cold, moist treatment are those of the black ash, bald cypress, basswood, some junipers, Osage orange, Digger pine, whitebark pine, Eastern redbud and yew.

● Generally speaking, seeds with a hard shell or pit require more "rest" before germinating than those with a softer shell or without a shell.

● Soft or fleshy seeds will usually grow almost immediately as soon as they are put in a suitable environment for germination. They should not be allowed to dry out.

● Citrus seeds will lose their vitality if they become too dry. They should be washed and planted immediately.

● Seeds from stone fruits (peaches, apricots, cherries, etc.) need to be washed free of fruit parts and juice as soon as possible. They lose their ability to germinate if they are allowed to ferment in fruit juice.

● To catch the seeds from pine cones, choose a cone that has turned a ripe brown on the tree but is still closed. Warm it in an oven set on low temperature (90 degrees F.) for several hours. The cone will open up so that the seeds can drop out. If the first warming isn't enough to open the cone, repeat; or else (if there are objections that the oven is on too long!) keep the cone in as warm a place as you can, such as near the radiator or next to the oven, until the cone does open.

Once your seeds have germinated and are up and growing, you can carry most of them along in the house—even tree seedlings, and even through the winter—with just normal care: temperatures on the cool side if you can manage it, water when the soil is dry, and enough light and sun.

Later on, the following spring, if your child has no spot of his own in which to plant his new trees, see if he can take them to school or to the park to plant. Be sure, too, that provisions are made for protection and follow-up care of the trees until they are well established.

Here is how to plant a tree, according to one of the world's greatest experts. (See Following Famous Scientists, page 99.) John Burroughs wrote this advice to a class of schoolchildren:

"When you plant a tree with love, it always lives, you do it with such care and thoroughness.

"Give the tree roots plenty of room and a soft, deep bed to rest in; tuck it up carefully with your hands. The roots of the tree are much more soft and tender than its branches and cannot be handled too gently."

The Jewish festival of the New Year of Trees, Tu B'shvat, celebrated usually in the latter part of January, is a wonderful time to encourage the planting of trees in your own yard, or in the yard of the synagogue or church. Of course, January is not always ideal tree-planting time in some parts of this country, but if you live in

159

the Southern sections or where the ground is not frozen, a mild January day is a very good time to set out fruit trees.

If you should have the opportunity to visit Israel, you may want to follow the example of thousands of other pilgrims and plant a tree there. (Leviticus 19:23 — "And when ye shall come into the land, and shall have planted all manner of trees . . .") Over a hundred million trees have been planted in Israel through the Jewish National Fund. Special tours will take you to one of nine main forests where you can plant the tree yourself. You will be given a tag upon which is written the location of your tree and on subsequent trips to Israel you may visit it.

If it's not likely that you can make such a trip, you can still arrange to have a tree—or for that matter, a garden of trees or even a forest of trees—planted in your name. The Jewish Community Center in your community will be able to give you more details.

Also, find out the date for Arbor Day in your state (see Arbor Days, page 239) and plan to plant a tree that day—especially if it's a tree you have started yourself from a seed you've found along the way. Arbor Day began in 1872 in the State of Nebraska to encourage people to plant trees, and more than a million were planted on that first Arbor Day. Now, more than a hundred years later, it is probably more important than ever that people plant trees—not simply for their usefulness after they are grown and harvested, but for the beauty they bring to our lives and the importance they play in cleansing our air. The fact is we must have trees, and lots of them, to survive. Plant as many trees as you can.

Look up your state tree (page 238) and see if you can determine its special significance to your state. The piñon pine of New Mexico and the single-leaf piñon of Nevada both have nutlike seeds which were an important part of the Indian diet. The maple is Vermont's tree, for its syrup and sugar; the Texas pecan, for food and wood; Virginia's flowering dogwood, for making the month of April unforgettably beautiful.

If you have moved about a bit as many families have, you will already have had the opportunity to know a number of different state trees and can appreciate their special significance in each of their own areas. Wherever you live, try to find some of your state tree's seeds along the way and see if you can get them to grow for you.

Seed-Package Artistry

Seeds, as we have seen, come in many different kinds of packages—packages designed by nature as a special protection for each kind of seed. Shells, pods, fruits, hulls, rinds—all are part of the protective packaging of seeds.

These seed packages themselves can be a special plus when looking for seeds along the way. Their shapes and sizes and designs provide infinite variety for the collector—whether acquired in one afternoon's outing or over a lifetime.

From spring through fall, especially, keep the seed packages in mind when you are out walking. Look for sycamore balls, pine cones, milkweed pods, the sweetgum's star-studded balls, the fragile lanterns of the winter cherry, the leathery pods of the buckeye, the acorns of the oak—all waiting for the collector's eye to light upon them.

At home, you can affix them to poster board, with identifying names written below. Or use a styrofoam tray, such as the kind meat is packaged on, to display the pods. Name tags can be written on paper and pasted on the tray next to the pods. Mosaics can be created by attaching the pods on the trays in a free-form or picture design.

Pine cones are fun to use in Thanksgiving and Christmas arrangements. When that first turkey picture comes home from school, your child can use it to draw another turkey head on to cardboard or construction paper to fit on a pine-cone body. Attach pipe-cleaner legs and the turkey is ready to go back to school the next day to show to classmates. A collection of them will make fine place cards for Thanksgiving dinner.

Sycamore and sweetgum balls for Christmas-tree ornaments: Gather them from the ground where they have fallen or cut them from the tree. If you pull them, the stems will come off. Spray with lacquer, sprinkle with glitter and hang by a string.

Fresh flower frogs: Use the colorful Osage orange to display fall leaves. Make holes in top only (if on sides, the sticky fluid inside can leak out) with an ice pick. Insert small branches of leaves into holes.

Acorn people can be made by joining acorns together with wire; walnut shells can be used as tiny flowerpots, and peanut shells as finger puppets. A pussywillow bud can become a bumblebee; a fat brown bur, a small porcupine.

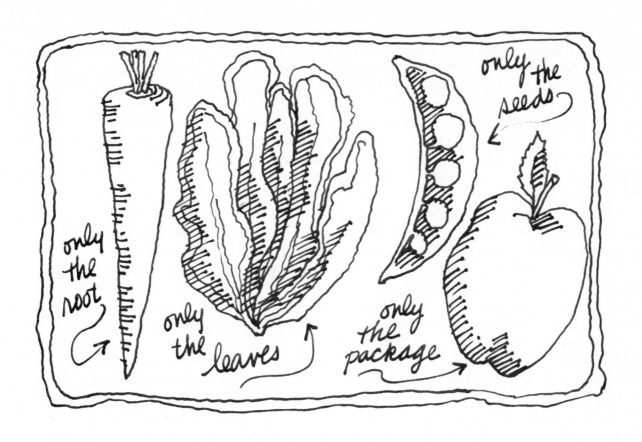

only the root

only the leaves

only the package

only the seeds

SUDDEN GREENERY FROM THE KITCHEN

For discovering gardening opportunities on a day-to-day basis, there is no better place than your own kitchen.

Mealtimes can bring discovery of many different plants and the parts of them that we eat. Children are often a bit taken aback when they realize that their dinner

163

is not just "food" but that a good part of it is made up of seeds, roots and leaves.

Your wondering aloud where a carrot's seeds are may prompt children to take a closer look at a carrot. And once you've posed the question, plant carrot seeds from a packet and then let the answer develop in the garden by allowing a few carrot plants to remain undisturbed until the tops flower and seed heads form. Meantime, point out that carrots are one of many vegetables—your child will be able to think of others—which we eat "mid-cycle," savoring the tender roots rather than the seeds. If your child samples the carrots after they have remained in the ground until the seed-bearing stage, he will see that eating the roots while they are tender is a better idea.

"Think of" games are a fun way to bring awareness. Can you think of some plants of which we eat just the seeds and throw away the "package"? (Beans, peas.) Can you think of some plants of which we eat just the package and throw away the seeds? (Peaches, apples.) Can you think of some plants of which we eat both the seeds and the package? (Squash, tomatoes.) Of which we eat everything between the seeds and the package? (Melons.) Of which we eat just the leaves? (Lettuce, cabbage.) Or the roots? (Carrots, radishes.)

Encourage your child to make a more extensive food-plant study. Each page of a scrapbook could have the picture of a vegetable or fruit dish as it appears on the dining table and a picture of the plant part from which it is prepared. He can sort through the seed catalogs for reminders and information, and clip pictures to illustrate his findings. Such a study can be expanded to include the grains (wheat, oats) and the seasonings (pepper, mustard) and even the drinks made from seeds (coffee, cola, cocoa).

A study of seeds by size can occupy a young mind for hours. The largest seed—what is it? And how large is it? The smallest and how small? More than the seed catalog will be required here. The local library and garden reference books will divulge the answers.

A companion study of the plants we eat for food would be one of seeds and plants that we must avoid. Far from growing up green, we would not grow up at all were we to partake of some common plants.

164

Plant poisoning causes deaths not only among livestock but among household pets, and children and adults as well. Every year thousands of people in the United States are victims of plant poisoning. Such a statement needn't frighten anyone away from the green life, but it should encourage us to be informed in order to inform others and thus reduce the number of accidental plant poisonings.

Some plants are toxic to touch, such as poison ivy, sumac and oak, and others are poisonous when taken internally. Parents may not be aware that some decorative plants used at Christmastime can be a possible hazard if very young children or animals are allowed unguarded access to them. The leaves and stems of the poinsettia are sometimes toxic and the berries of mistletoe and holly are poisonous if eaten.

A seed study of poisonous plants can be an extremely useful home and school endeavor, and will also help satisfy requirements for certain scouting badges.

As for action gardening, suppose your young gardener were to plant a different kind of seed from the kitchen each week. Or suppose you plant at least one of every kind of seed that turns up in your kitchen in a one-week period.

In the first place, there will be many more than you might think. Besides the obvious orange and grapefruit seeds, the beans and apple seeds, what about green pepper, cucumber, corn, date, popping corn, cantaloupe, watermelon, and strawberry seeds, as well as pecans, walnuts, and blueberries? There will be quite a lot of seeds to plant no matter what the season.

While you may soon wind up with a number of seed pots from such kitchen gardening, it needn't mean chaos. With just a little organization you will have a fascinating and informative garden venture going.

If you do not use the individual peat-pellet pots (see page 57), you can use small paper cups, the kind that come fifty to a package for about a dollar. You can assemble twenty-five to thirty of these on a single tray or shallow roasting pan. Punch a hole in the bottom of each cup for drainage and mark on the side of each the name of each seed planted therein and the date.

(If you go the peat-pellet route, the tops of aerosol cans make perfect individual containers for each peat pot; the name of the seed can be written on the side of the

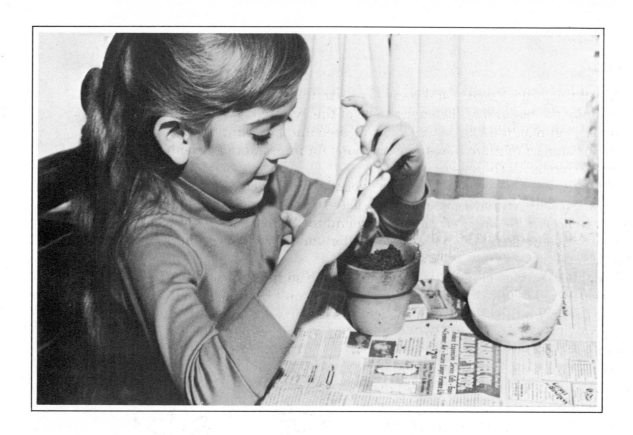

can-top with a felt marker, the small pots assembled on a tray to make it easier to tend them.)

If you have trouble germinating any of the seeds, see Seeds Along the Way, page 155.

A hint to get you started with the strawberry: the seeds are the little specks on the berry. Slice a berry in half; gently scoop out at least part of the fruit from the half; then flatten out the remainder, gently, cut-side down on a paper towel. Most of the fruit pulp and juice will now be eliminated. Place the limp little remains on a dish and leave them in a shaded area till barely dry, and the little specks will show up as seeds in their own right. These are what you plant.

Avocado

About the largest seed you'll come across in the kitchen is the avocado. Your children may not be fond of the subtle taste of the avocado (they'll wise up as they grow older), but no child can see an avocado seed and not want to plant it. It surely must be the subject of more how-to instructions for impromptu gardening than any other seed. Here is all there is to it:

When the seed is removed from the avocado, it is covered with a rather thick brown skin. It doesn't matter whether you leave this on or take it off. Just insert three toothpicks at about equal distance around the "waist" of the avocado seed. Place it pointed-end up in a glass of water and suspend it from the rim by the toothpicks.

Keep the water level in the glass high enough so that the bottom of the seed is always covered, adding water as it evaporates. Don't be concerned if a slimy coating appears on the seed and in the water. Just rinse the seed off and replace it in a glass of fresh water. (Adding a few pebbles of charcoal to the water discourages slimy happenings.)

add charcoal

As for how long it takes the seed to root, that's anybody's guess. Occasionally you will find an avocado with a seed almost at the sprouting stage. Other seeds will take a week or so to send down a root, and still others will sit in the glass week after week until the seed finally splits apart and the root emerges.

Next, a green shoot slowly emerges from the top of the seed, and after it reaches about 1 inch, things begin to move along at a faster pace. In a few days the shoot will be 3 or 4 inches tall, and the seed can be potted up.

Avocados can't take cold temperature, but they do quite nicely in the house with ordinary house-plant care. The avocado will head straight for the ceiling unless you or the children intervene. If you decide you would prefer a bushier plant, then pluck up your courage and when the avocado is a couple of feet high, whack off about one third of it. It will take a while, but new growth will appear along the sides of the stalk, and the plant will be off and growing again, and this time branching out instead of simply up.

Hanging Vegetable Roots

There are other ways to get a garden growing than starting from seed. Root crops, for example, make fast and easy growth. They will satisfy the most impatient of young gardeners.

Carrot leaves are lacy and bright green. Beets have large, dark green leaves veined with deep red. Turnip leaves are curly and apple-green. When you buy all of these vegetables in the grocery store, they are actually in between their first and second year of life. In the first year the plant forms the root. It is in the second year that they flower, seed and reproduce themselves. Obviously, most of them never make it to the second year because we eat them first.

You can give these vegetables a new lease on life and see them through to their full destiny, and in the doing have some fun and greenery from them.

Turnips, beets and rutabagas make the best root crops for little hanging baskets that will produce their own greenery. Carrots, and even radishes, will work, but they are so small and dry out so quickly that they must be refilled with water a number of times a day and will likely turn out to be a big pain in the neck for you and your child. So stick to the bigger roots to make your hanging basket.

A nice fat turnip is a good choice. Hollow it out from the pointed end; the flattened end, or what is thought of as the "top," is where the new leaves will come from. Push half of a round toothpick into each of three sides of the turnip, but not all the way in. Tie heavy thread to each toothpick end and knot together at the top. Now the turnip can be suspended as its own hanging basket.

The hollow must be kept filled with water, and since it is used up quickly by the turnip, it will need to be replaced a couple of times a day. Keep a glass of water nearby to eliminate trips back and forth to more distant parts of the house. A plastic cup works well because it can be squeezed to make its own pouring spout to get the water into the hollow. Small children like to convey the water from the glass to the turnip via a medicine dropper or a kitchen baster.

New leaves will sprout out quickly from what is now the turnip's bottom, and they will soon curl around the base and begin to grow upward. (A tropism at work; see pages 77-83.) Such roots make lovely and appealing little living baskets and are worth the trouble of keeping watered. When the leaves are growing well you can add potting soil to the inside of the turnip and sow cress or mustard seed there for a crop within a crop. (See page 137.)

Keep your turnip growing to reach the flowering and seed stage, and you will find it satisfying to participate in the "from generation unto generation" part of a plant's life that we ordinarily never see or give a thought to.

Besides hanging the roots of turnips, beets, or rutabagas, you can simply slice an inch or so off the large ends and plant these, cut-ends down, in potting soil. The same is true for carrots and radishes. Water them thoroughly and place in a sunny windowsill.

Still another way with roots: In a pan an inch or so deep, spread a half-inch layer of soil. Place about in the tray the cut-off tops of root vegetables—carrots, radishes, turnips, a sampling of different kinds; cover them all around with pebbles (colored ones from the dime store appeal to children and can be used over and over in different gardening ventures, such as forcing bulbs, dish gardens and so on). Water well, and watch the new foliage come up quickly for a whole trayful of kitchen greenery.

Sweet Potato

Like other members of the morning-glory family, the sweet potato grows as a beautiful twining vine. It's a speedy performer, too. You can start the vine from a sweet potato purchased from the supermarket. Insert three toothpicks around the midsection of the potato and put it in a water-filled jar so that the toothpicks rest on the rim. Place in a north window where it will get light but not direct sun. Add water as needed to keep the level near the top of the jar.

In three or four days, roots will begin to grow at the bottom of the potato, and a few days later leaves will appear at the top of it. As the vines grow, they can be trained to frame a window or kept pinched back to be a bushy house plant.

But the key word for kids with sweet potatoes is "training," which can mean growing the vines up along the spokes of a child's parasol that has seen its last days as a rain protector. With the potato jar below and the parasol's bare spokes outspread above, the vines can be trained to form a leafy bower.

A piece of chicken wire can be shaped as a ball to cover the jar and the vines trained in and out of it. The trouble with chicken wire is that almost no one ever has a stray piece of it lying around anymore, waiting to be used. But if you have old electric cords that can be opened up and the wire used, the kids can figure out their own weird ways of rigging up a challenge for the sturdy, dauntless sweet-potato vine.

Pineapple

After planting roots such as carrots and turnips, try your hand at planting tops. It is not difficult to interest a child who has just enjoyed the tangy fruit of the pineapple in planting its top to see if he can get another pineapple out of it! And the top does root quickly, grows without special care, and can be encouraged to produce fruit—all the while making an attractive house plant.

A faster route to rooting it than to cut off the top along with about 1 inch of the fruit (which is often recommended) is to simply twist off the top part, that is, the stem and its leaves. Then remove the lower leaves, exposing the stem for 1½ to 2 inches. Place the top in a small glass and fill with water up to the lowest remaining leaves. Add water as needed to maintain this level.

Within a week, you will be able to observe the first roots forming. When the glass is about half filled with strong, healthy roots, the top should be

transplanted to soil.

An ordinary clay flowerpot is best for the plant now. Put a piece of broken crockery over the drainage hole and fill the pot with a fertile, coarse soil. One part ordinary garden dirt and one part vermiculite is good. If you have peat moss, compost or leaf mold on hand, use it. The plant will thrive at temperatures above 60 degrees F. and in a highly humid atmosphere.

171

Inducing the plant to bloom requires a special but easy trick. Simply put the plant in a large plastic bag, add a ripe apple and twist the bag closed. Do not disturb for five days. The apple will be releasing ethylene gas as it ferments and that's the signal that turns the pineapple plant on.

Now you can remove the plant from the bag and resume normal care. Within two and a half to three months, the pineapple will be flowering. Keep up the good care, and from the flowering will come a baby pineapple—a sight to charm any young gardener.

Bulbs

Food also comes from bulbs—onions and garlic, for example. Select a clove from a bulb of garlic that is still fat and plump, not shriveled and dry. Suspend with toothpicks, flat-end down, in a glass or saucer of water (as with the avocado).

With garlic, the action is so fast that you can very nearly stand around and watch it grow. The roots and top of garlic are as robust as the aroma. The children should by all means make a growth chart, for they can record 6 or more inches of growth within three or four days.

6 Collecting Your Favorite Things

The desire to "collect" turns up in earliest childhood. From marbles all of one color to rocks of all kinds; from seashells at the beach to baseball cards in bubblegum packages—kids like to collect things.

A seldom thought of—but enormously rewarding—collection can be built around living plants. The beginnings of a collection can often be acquired by a child at the dime store for little more than a dollar. From there, he can go on to add plants found on trips or bought as vacation souvenirs. He can spot a new variety he'd like in a catalog. He can learn how to increase his plant holdings (see Making More from One, page 69) and then trade specimens with other collector friends. As his interest grows beyond what is easily accessible, he can look for new sources of information and plant material from the library, botanic gardens, specialty catalogs.

CACTI, FERNS, HERBS

A good way to begin a child's plant collection is to encourage him to concentrate on one type or family of plants. Ferns, herbs and succulents such as cacti, for example, are three of the many possibilities.

Cactus Plants and Other Succulents

Cacti are only one of a number of families of plants whose members have fleshy structures designed to hold water for long periods to tide them over the dry times. These types of plants are generally referred to as succulents, with members of the cacti family being the best known.

Cactus plants have never gotten a whole lot of attention either from plant lovers or would-be gardeners. Their image, unfortunately, is not a very good one. A person is inclined to think of a cactus, if he thinks of it at all, as one of the least attractive forms of plant life, offering little by way of color or form and rather too much in the way of spikes and spines.

Well, cacti deserve better than this, and no one is more likely to give them their due than children. And having done so, they and their parents will discover that the cactus family numbers among its members some startlingly beautiful plants; that many of them produce large, showy blooms; that they can be dramatic, exotic, amusing and, most of all, fun and easy to grow.

In addition to the above virtues, most cacti are also easy to propagate (see page 101). And the collector can create his own unique types of cacti by grafting—an art that with most other types of plants requires a good bit of knowledge, experience, patience and painstaking work. With cactus, it's not all that big a deal. (See Following Famous Scientists, Burbank, page 100.)

A cactus collection also combines well with other collectibles of childhood. Rocks, shells and the wide variety of simply neat things that children pick up along the way—a bird feather, a smooth twig or branch, a seed pod, the wishbone from Sunday's roast chicken!

Cacti also make good roommates for children. Their unusual shapes provide the same sort of daydreamy fun as cloud-gazing or shadow-watching—deciding that the round-shaped cactus with the two little sprouts at the top resembles a rabbit, and then one day as new growth pokes out at the base, it has suddenly become a balky donkey sitting back on its heels. Cacti are also agreeable things, not too demanding in their needs, and if someone forgets to water them for a week, they can survive with no hard feelings.

A cactus collection also combines well with other collectibles of childhood. Rocks, shells and the wide variety of simply neat things that children pick up along the way—a bird feather, a smooth twig or branch, a seed pod, the wishbone from Sunday's roast chicken!

Some tips on cactus care:

1. The cactus likes a sunny location.
2. Its soil should never be wet or soggy.
3. Give it some water and food during its growing season—twice a week for water, once a month for food. A tomato food is fine.
4. Water from the top, not the bottom, but don't wet the leaves and don't let

the plant stand in water. Whatever water drains through, pour off.

5. During the nongrowing season, think "desert" conditions, and lay off the water. Give it a drink only every two or three weeks and in the morning so that the plant will be dry by nighttime. Its resting period (when you will see no new growth or flowering) lasts about three or four months.

6. Small containers are best for cacti—to lessen the chances of overwatering. In a big pot the soil will take longer to dry out and the plant roots will remain wet longer.

7. Plant in a soil that is at least half sandy, so it will be loose and well drained.

Some types:

Opuntia. This is the kind of cactus seen so commonly on dime-store plant counters. Their flat oval or round pads will produce "ears" that gradually grow into more pads producing more "ears" as well as "tails," "horns," and other appendages, depending upon what one imagines the plant resembles at any given stage. The prickly pears belong to this family of cacti.

Mammillaria. There are more than two hundred species here. These often have the tall and cylindrical or globular spiny shapes that many people think of when they think cactus. They are great plants for kids, attractive and easy to grow and good candidates for grafting.

Peanut cactus. This is a natural for children to grow. It produces lots of large, scarlet-colored flowers in the spring. The plant itself is small, with low-branching stems, and the flower seemingly cupped within another flower is striking against the pale green, spiny stems.

Old man cactus. A surprise for most children because instead of spines, the plant is covered with long white hairs. You can start out with a small 2-inch-high plant and wind up with one the size of a large fruit jar.

Christmas cactus. If it is to bloom at Christmas, beginning about the first week of November it needs to be in a sunny spot in a room that isn't too brightly lit at night. It simply isn't true that no ray of light must hit it at night and that it must be tucked away in a closet every night at six for six weeks in order to bloom. To come into bloom it does need a lot of light during the day and no sustained bright light at night.

How to increase your cactus collection:

1. If the plant has branches or plantlets or pads, take a whole segment for a rooting.
2. If the plant's stems are jointed, take enough of the stem to include at least one joint.
3. If the plant is a tall columnar type, simply cut a piece off the top of it.
4. If the plant has a long unjointed stem, the stem can be cut into several pieces for rootings.
5. After you have cut off from the plant the piece to be rooted, put it aside for a few days in a shady place to let the cut edges dry out. (If you have cut several pieces from one stem, mark the edge of the bottom side of each with a tiny piece of tape or with a Magic Marker so you don't forget which end is which. The bottom side is what goes into the soil to root.)
6. Let the cut edges dry completely before putting the piece in a pot to root.
7. Fill the pot with soil mix, except for the top inch. Here put in a layer of sand or vermiculite for the cutting to root in.
8. Push the cutting into the rooting mixture only about a half inch deep. Moisten but don't overwater. As the roots form on the cutting, they will reach down into the potting mixture and a new plant will be off and growing on its own.

JADE TREE (CRASSULA ARGENTEA)

A succulent, not a member of the cactus family, but an absolute must for children. One of the most interesting plants a child can have because it is so much like a tree—a strange, fascinating one indeed. The stem becomes a thick, reddish-brown, barklike trunk with almost a petrified-forest appearance about it. If you take cuttings from the tree, it branches more. It can be made to grow in a completely symmetrical form, or it will branch into graceful, flowing shapes. If the main branch is cut off flat at the top, new growth will appear at the very edge of the cut part and a new branching effect will begin, and/or new shoots will come up at the base of the "tree."

Ferns

Ferns make splendid plants for collecting because there are so many different kinds, all with beautiful colors and shapes yet differing greatly one from another. A fern collection also provides the source for a beautiful nature book. (See Sharing the Designs in Nature, page 203.)

In mounting or placing fern specimens in a nature book, the large fronds can be broken partway down from the top to fit the page, and the top part reversed in an upside down V shape to show the underside. Select a fertile frond, that is, a leaf with spore cases (see below), and these will then show when you reverse the top part. Plan to include a small, newly emerged fiddlehead, too, to make your collection more complete.

Ferns aren't reproduced from seeds but from spores. You can grow these spores yourself to see the little plant, called the prothallium, that comes between the two generations of ferns. This plant is so tiny that many of even the most avid gardeners have never seen one. The biggest they ever become is about a quarter inch.

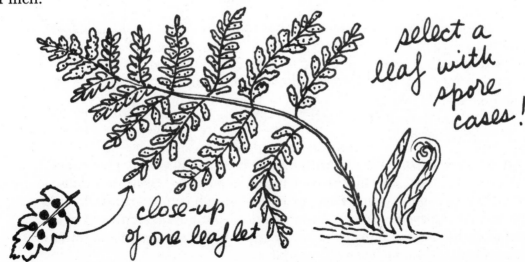

select a leaf with spore cases!

close-up of one leaflet

Here's how to grow your fern spores, and from these you can cultivate new ferns for trading with other collectors and for giving as delightful gifts.

1. On the back of some of the fronds (leaves) of a mature fern, small greenish spots will begin to appear. These are spore cases.
2. When you see these spots, keep watch as they develop into small brown or golden dots. (They will look like tiny insects of some sort clinging to the undersides of the leaves.) The spore cases are then ripe and about ready to burst.
3. Break off the frond, place it spore-side down on a piece of paper and put it where it won't be disturbed at all for a few days.
4. Fill a pot with a mixture of peat moss and sand and top with a layer of sand. Wet thoroughly.
5. Lift the fern from the paper. Look closely (super closely) to see the very, very fine specks that have fallen onto the paper. These are the spores. Scrape off any spore cases that remain on the fern frond; you can give these a gentle jab with a needle to open them. Then dust the whole business over the moistened sand.
6. Cover with a piece of clear plastic wrap. Put in a warm, light place. To keep the sand moist, water from the bottom so as not to disturb the tiny spores. Within a few weeks, thin green threads will appear, followed by the tiny, heart-shaped prothallia. They are so small at the beginning that you may notice, even on careful looking, only a slightly green haze on the surface of the sand. But from these small plants will come the new ferns that will resemble their grandparents.

Another way you can encourage your ferns to reproduce themselves, and provide you with the most new plants for the least amount of time and effort on your part, is simply to plant your original fern plant in a container larger than it actually needs. As the spore seeds ripen on the plant and burst, some of the spore dust will land on the open soil in the pot. You'll not likely see the little prothallia in this case, but eventually new ferns will develop.

In addition, some ferns can be propagated from the runners they put out, which send up new shoots. The large pot also provides room for these runners to find new growing sites. Either way, as time goes by you will have a number of baby ferns to take up and transplant to other pots. For a large, showy fern pot of your own, leave a number of the ferns growing in one large pot to fill it entirely with their graceful fronds.

Here are some ferns that are easy to grow indoors and that would make an enviable collection:

African ruffly fern or Florida ruffle fern.   This plant has small, graceful fronds and a light green, fluffy look to it.

Australian bracken or trembling brake fern.   Children will like this fern because it is a fast grower and always has lots of new fiddleheads coming up.

Bird's-nest fern. This plant has shining, broad-leaved green foliage that spreads out from the crown to form the "bird's nest." It is fun to have in a fern collection because it doesn't look at all like a fern!

Maidenhair fern.   The separate parts of these fern fronds look like tiny fans. This is a very delicate, lacy fern, but it is a sturdy grower, easy to care for, and will grow old along with you.

Button fern.   The little round leaf parts of this fern grow low and spreading and make for a lovely hanging-basket plant. Even while it is still young and tiny, you will enjoy fixing a small hanging basket for it. Hang it low, though, so that you can see this lovely little gray-green fern.

Boston fern.   This was the most popular house plant of great-grandmother's day. Everybody owned one, or wanted to, back in the gay nineties. It came from a chance mutation and was first sold by a florist in Boston. It can be propagated easily by cutting off a runner bud from the parent plant and potting it up.

Staghorn fern.   Once you become a fern collector, it will probably be your ambition to own one of these fascinating plants. They look nothing at all the way ferns are supposed to look, but instead their leaves (the fertile ones) are shaped like the antlers of a big deer. There are many different types of staghorn ferns—some

181

big, some small—but they grow slowly, so that even the large types are suitable for house plants.

Fern asparagus. This is the spidery, lacy type with prickles on the stem. One of the most delicate of all the ferns, it is the one that is often included with cut roses from the florist. It is a good choice to include in a child's collection to add to the range of fern shapes and textures.

Herbs

Instead of being labeled simply an herb collection, why not a taste-and-smell plant collection? Children enjoy collecting herbs as much for their aroma as for the other uses that can be made of them, and the name of this collection has just enough irreverence to add to the fun.

Candy and chewing-gum smells coming from plants? Spearmint and peppermint.

A plant that conjures up Thanksgiving and roast stuffed turkey? Sage.

And that familiar clean, fresh scent so widely used these days in everything from furniture polish to bowl cleaners? Lemon balm.

An herb collection can be housed in interesting ways for children. A small strawberry jar or a small keg made according to directions for the strawberry barrel (see page 130) provides a lot of anticipation if the plants are acquired one by one and the container gradually fills with a new and different occupant for each pocket.

Many herb enthusiasts believe that nothing but clay pots will do for their herbs—for appearance as much as for their culture. This can be a sort of status-in-reverse decision that might close down lots of other creative potting arrangements a child would choose for his collection. One child might enjoy very much tailor-making a pot, or cachepot, for each herb, with the container for each plant bearing its own distinctive and appropriate artwork—a painted design, or a fabric or other covering, or decoupages from magazines or catalogs.

Another collector might prefer that all the pots match, but still be pots he has chosen himself—whether clear plastic pots or a set of coffee cans all painted the same color.

One more word: If the collection truly belongs to the child, whether it is housed on a sunny windowsill in his bedroom or in the kitchen, he will be interested in knowing about those occasions when a cook other than himself has harvested some of the fresh herbs. "Used some of your parsley in the lentil soup I made today" will not only add to the appreciation of the soup but to the child's pride of stewardship. Obviously, if he is around when the harvesting is to take place, he can assist in making decisions on which and how much to snip off.

The following are herbs any child would enjoy collecting. Some will appeal particularly to the beginning chef who will enjoy learning to put them to use. All are exceptionally handsome plants and most are generous in their growth habits—of no small importance to children. One exception is the slow-growing English thyme. But its tiny leaves on a quaint-looking miniature shrub will mark it for special affection as the runt of the collection.

PARSLEY AND THYME AND ROAST STUFFED CHICKEN

You can start parsley from seeds or buy small plants from the nursery. There are so many uses for this curly green plant—and children often learn to like it as a fresh nibble to pick while passing by—that it is worth having several plants. If planting in a strawberry jar, save parsley for the top. Makes a lovely green crown, and it needs the room to branch out.

Thyme makes a tiny bush, with very small leaves on woody branches that grow all in a tangle. Save one of the top pockets of the strawberry jar for this herb. Children will enjoy snipping off a small branch and then snipping several of its leaves straight from the branch into their soup!

Here's a recipe for a truly superb roast chicken that can nonetheless be put together by a pint-sized cook with only a bit of help the first time round to get the hang of how to stuff and truss the bird. From then on, when the herb collection shows a good-sized amount of parsley on hand and a bit of thyme, the family has a treat in store for them with this recipe:

Roast Stuffed Chicken*

Ingredients:
1 ready-to-cook roasting chicken
Half a lemon

Stuffing:
About ¾ cup (1½ sticks) butter
1 onion, peeled and minced
1 rib celery, chopped
15 to 20 parsley sprigs, minced

3 teaspoons fresh thyme, minced
   (or 1 teaspoon dried)
2½ cups fine, dry bread crumbs
Salt
Freshly ground pepper

Preheat the oven to 350 degrees (or moderate) for 15 minutes before placing the chicken in to roast.

Rub the inside of the chicken with the cut side of half a fresh lemon. Set bird aside.

Melt 6 tablespoons of the butter in a saucepan. Add the onion and ½ cup water. Cook over moderate heat until all the water has boiled away and the onion is limp and transparent. Combine with the celery, parsley, thyme, bread crumbs, 2 tablespoons of the butter (melted), and salt and pepper to taste. The stuffing should be moist but not soggy.

Stuff the chicken, fasten the opening with the metal skewers and truss. Place on a rack in a roasting pan. Rub the entire surface of the chicken well with the remaining butter, softened. Sprinkle lightly with salt and pepper.

Roast in the preheated oven, uncovered, for 1 hour and 20 to 30 minutes. Baste every 15 minutes with pan juices, using a bulb baster or long metal spoon. If there is not sufficient juice, add more melted butter. Test for doneness: the juices should run clear yellow when a drumstick is pierced at the thickest part with a fork and the leg should feel soft when squeezed.

Allow the chicken to "rest" 15 to 20 minutes after it comes from the oven. This allows juices to settle and makes carving easier.

*Helen McCully, *Cooking With Helen McCully Beside You* (New York: Random House, 1970).

SPEARMINT, PEPPERMINT AND CANDIED LEAVES

Both of these mints are musts for the young herb collector. They grow fast and can be pinched back often. Sprigs of either one can perk up and garnish iced tea and other summer coolers.

Candied mint leaves also make a big hit with children. When a birthday cake is called for, plan on candied mint leaves for part of the decoration. For special desserts, too.

To candy mint leaves (also rose or violet petals), here are two methods, both easy. The second is more suited to a small child and also takes a good bit less time and fuss.

One way: Make a syrup of 1 cup sugar and ½ cup water. Boil until it spins a thread. Remove from heat and cool. Pick perfect mint leaves (or rose or violet petals). Dip them one at a time into the syrup. The best way to dip, really, is with your fingers, so make *sure* the syrup is cooled—hot sugar syrup can burn like the dickens. Place on waxed paper and sprinkle with sugar. (Tint the sugar ahead of time, if you like, with the appropriate food color—green, pink or blue—for a pastel sugar coating to match the leaf.) Let leaves dry thoroughly.

Another way: Beat the white of an egg till it is foamy. Dip the petals into the egg white; shake to remove excess; spread on waxed paper; sprinkle with sugar; let dry; shake off excess sugar.

LEMON BALM AND SWEET BASIL—
FOR A FIRST COLLECTION

Lemon balm and sweet basil ought to be part of a kid's collection because parents will enjoy them so much.

Lemon balm is great to have around just as a friend. Its aroma is simply terrific. A sprig of it will also grace any glass of iced tea, and the leaves can make a fruit salad something special. For the youngest of cooks learning to use herbs, nothing could be easier than adding leaves of lemon balm to banana and orange slices.

Sweet basil must be a part of any gardener's household, if for no other reason than to team up with the fresh tomatoes that every gardener should be growing. The basil plant itself is extraordinarily attractive with its bright, crinkly leaves. The more it is pinched out, the better it likes it, and it will grow into a lovely fat plant.

The young owner can mince the leaves to sprinkle over fresh sliced tomatoes. There is scarcely a simpler way to learn about and enjoy the extra added something that herbs can bring to good eating.

CATNIP AND GROW YOUR OWN MOUSE

If you share your household with a cat as well as kids, then a pot of catnip belongs in your herb collection, too. Homemade catnip toys can provide some lively taste-and-smell treats for the feline member of the family.

Catnip seed is widely available in garden stores and is often found on the seed racks of grocery and variety stores; it is also available through seed catalogs.

Plan to protect the young plants from kitty for the first few weeks; otherwise the entire project may be eaten before it gets off the ground. Give him a fresh sprig or two now and then, rather than letting him help himself, and the catnip plants will have a better chance of making it to adulthood.

Limit his snacks until the plants reach a height of about 1½ to 2 feet. Then you can break off a number of branches and hang them upside down in a cool, airy place to dry (or dry in the oven as on page 189). Then strip the leaves from the branches and gently crush them. This will be the "stuffing" for your catnip toys.

To make your catnip toys, choose a piece of sturdy material from the family's ragbag for the covering. A good catnip-mouse skin can be made out of a pair of old jeans (except for the knees and seat, of course, which would undoubtedly be too thin).

If you sew your catnip toy by hand, be sure to make tiny, strong stitches so that the catnip will not work out and so that kitty cannot easily tear it open.

186

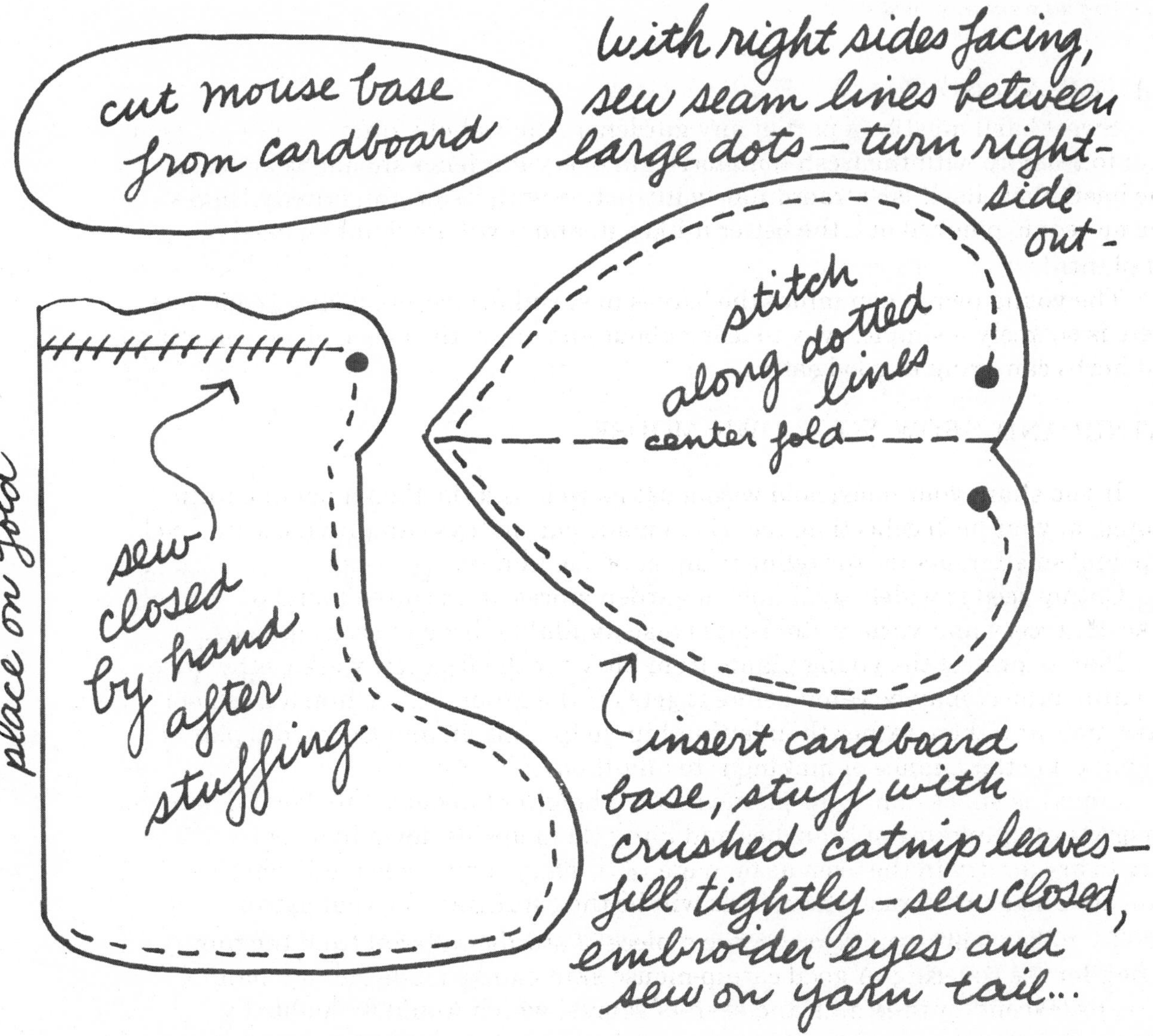

cut mouse base from cardboard

with right sides facing, sew seam lines between large dots — turn right-side out —

stitch along dotted lines

center fold

place on fold

sew closed by hand after stuffing

insert cardboard base, stuff with crushed catnip leaves — fill tightly — sew closed, embroider eyes and sew on yarn tail...

Make mouse, sock, Santa or other shapes for your cats, and some for your cat's cat friends, at Christmas, birthday and other gift-giving times.

CAMOMILE AND TEA WITH PETER RABBIT

Camomile is a low-growing, always green plant with flower stalks that grow as high as 12 inches. The flowers are daisylike, with white petal-like rays and yellow centers, and from these blossoms the tea is made.

Small children especially, and Beatrix Potter fans of any age, will enjoy a spot of camomile tea while having another look-and-read-through of *The Tale of Peter Rabbit.*

The tea was said to be good for nervousness, which would seem to be the proper prescription for Peter Rabbit after his harrowing encounter with Farmer McGregor.

How to Make Herb Tea

Pour 1½ cups (12 ounces) of boiling water over a good handful of blossoms —ten or twelve—or fresh leaves of other herbs. Cover and let steep for 10 minutes—not much longer, else you may get a bitter taste. Drink plain or sweeten with honey and add a squeeze of lemon juice.

Many herb-tea enthusiasts believe that the best teas are made when three or four different herbs are combined. Children usually subscribe to this theory. They like the mixing of this with that, and so long as they (and parents) know the identity of the plants they are brewing up, they can become discriminating tea tasters while growing their own herbs.

TO DRY HERBS

Have on hand a small jar with a tight-fitting lid—a baby-food jar, for example—to put the herb into as soon as it has been dried so that you preserve its aroma and flavor.

Snip off the branches to be dried and put on a dish, uncovered, in the refrigerator for a day or two. Be vigilant especially at this time to have other items in the refrigerator properly covered so that no transfer of aroma from the herbs takes place. When the herb leaves have gone completely limp, they are ready to finish off drying.

Put the oven on the lowest temperature—barely warm. Pick the leaves off the branches and stems and spread the leaves out in a single layer on a shallow pan. (Discard branches and stems.) Slip the pan in the oven and leave just until the leaves dry and crisp. It will likely take only a few minutes, and don't, for heaven's sake, heat up the oven to rush things. Keep it barely warm! When the leaves crumble easily between your fingers, remove from the oven, crumble and put into the jar.

BONSAI

Introduce your child early to tree collecting and you have made a bonsai fan for life. The subject of bonsai—that ancient oriental art form which captures the life forces of a tree in a small flat dish—is irresistibly intriguing to child and adult alike.

This very beautiful aspect of gardening receives only the briefest of introductions here. Some enthusiasts have devoted whole lifetimes to the subject, and the purists will hotly debate the finest details of bonsai tradition. Don't assume, however, that there is some snobbery inherent in the subject and let that put you off from plunging in on your own, learning and studying more as you go, and sharing the collecting of bonsai with your children.

Time and your own experience will determine whether you and/or your child will become a nut about bonsai. All gardeners have at least one specialty they do go nutty over—some remaining faithful to one love all their lives and others moving from one collection to another through the years. If bonsai turns out to be one of your family's collectibles, you have many hours of learning and patience ahead of you and great rewards in the joy and beauty your miniature trees will bring you.

A good way to begin a child's bonsai collection is with a tree that is as old as he is—one that can celebrate birthdays right along with him, the two growing up together.

If your child is five and you didn't plant a seedling tree at his birth, no reason not to begin with a five-year-old tree and dub its birthday to coincide with your child's.

Look in garden shops or nurseries for plants being sold in containers—anywhere from 1- to 5-gallon cans. Those that are intended for landscape plantings usually make the best buys. In addition, the ones that make the best bonsai are likely to be the ones that have been passed over by shoppers because they are misshapen or scrubby-looking or not as large as their companions. The reject may have the gnarled roots, the interesting twist to its trunk, the stunted growth, that will make a great bonsai beginning—and it may even be marked down in price, too!

The types of trees for bonsai are almost limitless. Probably the best known are junipers, pines, firs and cypresses. But other plants also do well: the azalea, flowering quince, cherry, peach, birch, beech, camellia, pittosporum, aralia and pyracantha are just a few.

1. Ask to have the can cut before you take it home so that the plant can be dumped out easily.

2. Spread out newspapers for a work surface and have a bucket of water handy.

3. Spread out the branches to get a good look at the main trunk line and the possibilities for shaping. A good pattern for the youngster to follow with a first bonsai is the one from *ikebana:* the lines of Heaven, Man and Earth. Heaven the highest branch, Earth the lowest, and Man in between—with the latter two both turned toward Heaven. (See Flower Arranging, page 217.)

4. Before cutting any branches, decide which ones will stay, which ones will go. Use bright-colored twistum and mark the branches you want to keep so that when you are caught up in the actual pruning, you don't make a fatal mistake and whack off the wrong branch.

5. Let your child help choose branches that best represent Heaven, Earth and Man. In making decisions, keep in mind that the lowest branches usually will be first on the list to go so that the main trunk will be exposed. Branches that cross to the inside also should be eliminated to open up the design. Branches that grow out away from the center are the ones to save. It may be, though, that you will want to work with a wayward branch, training it with wire to bend or twist for the eventual effect you want.

6. In pruning, cut the branches off close to the trunk so that no stumps are left showing. With the side of a scissors' blade or a small sharp knife, carefully and *gently* scrape away at the pruning site, leaving a small indentation that will eventually scar over. No part of your tree should be left with a rude stump that will proclaim for years afterward, "I was pruned!"

7. If the plant has a knobby, gnarled root cap at the base of the trunk, plan to leave this showing above ground when you replant, to add a highly prized interest to the planting.

Now for the roots:
1. Remove as much of the soil as you can by gently untangling the roots that

show and shaking the plant gently. Then dunk the roots in the bucket of water and let soak for a few minutes to loosen the rest of the soil. Now you will be able to see the whole of the root system you are working with.

2. If the roots are heavy and matted, you will need to prune heavily. If there seems to be much more soil than roots, then go easy on the pruning. Cut back on the long, heavy roots to encourage fine feeder roots to grow. Be as gentle as possible with the tiny roots already there.

3. Snip back about a third of the roots. Parents often shrink from this job. Children seem to love it. (You are left to decide for yourself what this bit of sociology may mean in terms of the human condition.)

4. You will want to dip the roots into the water from time to time to keep them from drying out while you are working on them and agonizing over the decisions.

5. If your plant is a large one, don't try to make the jump from a 5-gallon container to a small bonsai dish in one branch-and-root-whacking session. Be content to take the one third off the roots; settle the plant into an intermediate-size container; let it recover for a few months (up to a year); and then repeat the pruning process again.

Potting:
1. Most traditional bonsai containers are plain clay dishes or pots in earthy tones of brown, green or gray, with plain, simple lines. However, glazed colors of blue, dull yellow and terra-cotta are often lovely when used for a flowering tree. The main thing is that the container not detract from the planting itself.

Children will enjoy choosing their bonsai containers because they are so different from other types of plant containers. The pots and dishes made especially for bonsai can be found in import stores at reasonably low prices; also in garden and nursery shops and sometimes in dime stores. The dishes have one or more drainage holes depending on the size. These holes are usually plugged with small plastic caps that should be punched out before planting—an obvious child activity.

2. Place a small piece of wire mesh—or an odd-shaped rock if it's easier to come by—over the hole so that water can drain out but not the soil with it. Some

bonsai experts say that no gravel layer need be provided so long as you have the drainage hole and the proper soil. However, plain old gardeners who have been brought up to protect their plants from wet feet at all costs will sleep better knowing their bonsai has a light layer of gravel to rest on. Besides, once you have taught the growing-green youngster to "always think good drainage layer" for plants, there's no sense undoing it.

3. Now the soil. Use what comes along with the plant, just ordinary dirt, mixed with leaf mold (available at nurseries, garden shops, in small-size bags) and sand or perlite. Proportions should be about half and half: one half dirt to one quarter sand or perlite plus one quarter leaf mold. You want a soil mix that is light enough to drain well but not so airy that the water will flush straight through. Most garden dirt by itself will be too heavy and will compact and hold moisture too long. Most potting mixes will be too light, and with the limited amount used in the bonsai container, will not retain moisture long enough. So go to the trouble of mixing this soil recipe, and the effort will be worth it to keep happy the plant that will become a long-time friend.

4. Don't be nervous about what may seem a very small amount of soil for the plant to live in. With good drainage and proper care, bonsai plants can live happily for years and years in only an inch or two of soil. Which is what provides much of the fascination for children.

Care and feeding:
1. Bonsai plants do not achieve their dwarfed state through starvation. The size comes from proper top and root pruning, and from confinement in a small pot. Feeding is essential to keep the plant alive and healthy.

2. Commercial house-plant foods of the type that are dissolved in water before use are fine for bonsai. Be careful not to make too strong a solution. Lean toward making a more dilute solution than the directions call for—certainly never stronger. Feed once a month beginning in the spring and carrying on through fall, and not at all during the winter months.

Finishing touches:

Let your child look for a very special rock or two; thin pieces of slate with ridges on the surface are especially good-looking with bonsai. A bent, twisted twig to place alongside the plant or a miniature orange pomander suits a bonsai arrangement perfectly. Soft, furry green moss also adds to the planting. If moss is not available, baby's tears or Corsican mint will make a lovely low-growing green carpet for bonsai. It will eventually trail over the edges of the container and may need to be pruned back, but this is not essential. Your child may prefer to let the baby's tears grow. And the bonsai, too, for that matter, as long as its growth remains consistent with the size the container is able to sustain. Eventually, more pruning of top and bottom may be needed, but these are decisions that can be arrived at over a long period of time.

Sometimes on outings a real treasure for bonsai may be discovered. A storm, a bulldozer or a poor environment has left what might have been a forest giant a small scraggly tree instead, apparently barely clinging to life. To all but the bonsai eye, it might seem a sorry sight indeed. Which is why it is worthwhile to train a young eye for a bonsai view—so that the child can see beauty's face in the adversities and hardships that abound in nature. The hard life the tree has endured is exactly what makes it so appealing as a candidate for the bonsai art.

(Before digging and making off with it, strictly observe the Code for Good Green People, page 233.)

Another approach to bonsai, and one of the most enjoyable for children, is the planting of a whole miniature forest of their own in a single bonsai container. They can begin with seeds or cuttings that they have started themselves. (See Making More from One, page 69, and Gardening Is Where You Find It, page 155.)

Quicker results can be obtained by buying small seedlings, though these are often offered only in large quantities, say, 25 to 50 seedlings to a package, through mail-order nurseries. Think twice before this deters you, however, for with such quantities your youngster might work up a lasting, worthwhile project for a neighborhood group, scout troop, or school class.

In planting a bonsai forest—a grove of maples, a stand of pine—follow potting directions outlined above. Plant the trees so they appear randomly placed as in nature. A few might be grouped together, for example, and others spaced more apart. As in *ikebana,* wind up with the parts of the arrangement—and the whole—in odd numbers.

Where to place:

Not in direct hot sun. Bonsai will do well in a window that receives good light but no direct sun at all.

The young bonsai owner may move his tree about as long as he remembers that too big a change all at once in environment—light, temperature, etc.—is not good for any plant. They hate it. (See The ABC's of Gardening, page 53.)

Postscript on bonsai:

Other places to keep an eye out for bonsai possibilities include your own yard. A shrub or bush that hasn't "done well"—one that has hung on for a few years, possibly gaining a fatter trunk but not much growth. This underachiever might be an excellent candidate for adding to the bonsai collection.

Let your youngster dig all around it, sinking the shovel in as deep as he can. The plant can then be left in the ground for a few months while it develops a compact root system. Or you can transfer it to a container and leave it for a few months before beginning to prune it to size for a bonsai container. If the plant is a large one, remember that it may take two or three pruning sessions spaced over several months each—with the size of the container also reduced each time you reduce the size of the plant—to get it down to bonsai proportions.

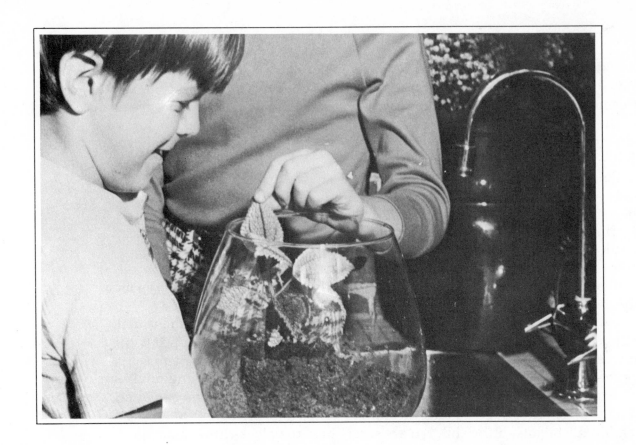

TERRARIUMS

Terrariums become an instant hobby for children when they are suggested as display cases for plant and nature collections.

The terrarium at school is often already fixed and waiting, so that the only action is in the looking. At home, a child can arrange and plant the terrarium to his

197

own tastes, and that's a big plus. It's an even bigger plus if he also has the chance to look for and collect the kind of plants and other stuff he wants to include in his terrarium. He very likely will wind up with a somewhat shaggier-looking terrarium than the preplanted sort you can buy, but consider this a major plus, too, for it is good for children to learn early that the best part of nature—your own involvement with it—is really not for the buying.

Plant collections can be housed in a glass-sided anything. Fish bowls or tanks, brandy snifters (large and small), old glass candy and apothecary jars or their modern counterparts, bottles of all kinds as long as the glass is clear so that you will be able to see the planting within. You'll need a cover for the top of the wide-mouthed containers, a glass saucer for the brandy snifter, a piece of window glass or Plexiglas for the fish tank. Bottles with narrow necks can get by without a top, but corks to fit are usually easily found and will help keep more of the moisture in.

Let your youngster have a say in choosing the container. Junk shops make good places for bottle-browsing. He might come across an animal-shaped bottle that was once used for soft drinks. As long as the bottle is clear so he can see the garden within, anything goes. A small bottle can make a charming miniature garden; a big bottle a dramatic one. In some of the import stores, you can often find huge glass water jugs—3 and 4 feet high. These make really great gardens for children's rooms—if the children are safely past the block-throwing stage and aren't given to violent roughhousing with their friends. Every parent knows deep down for which child a big glass bottle garden in his room would be an open invitation to disaster. For that child, and that parent, the small, solid, fish-tank type that sits safely back on a desk or dresser top might be indicated. But for a child who can live compatibly with a large bottle terrarium, it is well worth having. Plan to plant it in place because the completed garden will be heavy and difficult to move without disturbing the planting.

For the child with a scientific bent, laboratory glassware—beakers and flasks—make appealing terrarium containers. (Look in the Yellow Pages under Laboratory Equipment and Supplies.)

For the small child, a glass cheese dome or a clear glass salad bowl (which can also often be found in import stores at low prices) will be easier to work with. The plants can be arranged in any wide bowl—from cereal size to casserole—and little hands can move about freely. When the planting is completed, the clear glass dome is simply popped over the whole thing.

What you'll need: some small pebbles, some charcoal (briquettes can be broken up), loose, humusy soil or packaged potting soil, the plants, and an hour or two with a youngster who is eager to put a plant collection together.

Spread out newspapers for working. If the pebbles were picked up here and there, they might benefit from a washing, so let your child do this if he likes. (He will like.)

If he has chosen a tall, narrow-necked bottle, lay it on its side so that the pebbles can be rolled in to eliminate the risk of cracking a thin-glassed bottle. Roll in enough pebbles to cover the bottom of the bottle two or three layers thick when it's upright. Next comes a layer of charcoal.

For the soil, make a funnel by rolling a cone out of a piece of stiff paper (notebook or construction paper, etc.). Insert this three-fourths of the way into the bottle and then pour the soil in—to a depth of 1½ to 2 inches. The funnel keeps the soil from getting the insides of the bottle dirty. Any wayward bits of dirt can be wiped off with a paper towel wrapped securely around a long-handled fork or spoon, or a stick, and swished around a bit. It's easier, though, if you try not to get the bottle dirty to begin with. If some dirt does smear, then a very small amount of water poured in while you tilt the bottle and roll it gently back and forth should clean it.

Your child will like the idea of arranging the dirt in small hills and valleys rather than in just a flat layer, and the resulting landscape will be much more interesting visually. And then he is ready to plant.

For a bottle garden, use a long enough stick or spoon to reach in and poke a hole in the soil where you want each plant to grow. Then, in a sort of chopstick fashion (and chopsticks, if they are long enough, are good to use), pick up your plant by the stem, lower it gently through the opening, roots first, scootch it into

the planting hole and smooth the soil around it. Tamp the dirt down. If you haven't anything on hand to firm the soil with, try a large flat cork on the end of a pointed stick.

Don't be afraid to let the child move his plants around until he gets the collection settled the way he wants it. Let him look at the arrangement from all sides. He can prune back a plant if it is too tall or scraggly. Encourage him to look for straggling leaves to eliminate or a whole branch to remove rather than whacking off the top of a plant. Taking the plant's measure before it ever goes into the bottle helps, too, of course.

When all of the plants are settled in, moisten the whole business. Don't soak. For a narrow-necked bottle a kitchen baster is just the thing to apply a small amount of water evenly over the planting. For a wide-mouthed container, a sprayer from a window cleaner does a good job.

Now the terrarium is finished and it will need to rest in a shady spot for a few days. Then it can be put into place—in either natural or artificial light, but *not* in direct sunlight.

A few dead leaves are likely to appear soon after planting. This is no cause for alarm. Simply reach in and snip off (for tall bottles use a couple of long-handled spoons held together tweezer fashion) and remove. The plants will take hold, and while an occasional leaf will yellow from time to time, the main planting will thrive. Keep the arrangement clipped clean of sickly leaves to keep the looks of the terrarium in tiptop condition.

What kinds of plants to collect for terrariums?

For plants you buy, the major thing to remember is that the environment in your terrarium will be warm and moist. Therefore plants such as cactus and other succulents—which like things on the dry side—will not be good choices for the covered terrarium or narrow-necked bottle gardens.

Plants that do well in terrariums include miniature ivy, miniature roses, strawberry begonias, miniature African violets, miniature orchids, periwinkles *(Vinca minor)*, ferns, mosses. Many of these are often seen in dime stores and garden centers. Ferns make especially good fill-in plants. Choose a type, such as bracken or maidenhair, that does not grow too fast and does not send its fronds straight up high in the air.

Think of different kinds of effects in displaying the plant collection. For example, for the child with a romantic soul, consider a Victorian-type nosegay, using miniature African violets, with a pink for the plants circling the outside edge, a darker accent of deep lavender for the center, and a softening at the edges with a bit of fine fern. A large clear salad or punch bowl makes a beautiful enclosure for this arrangement.

A child with a love of mystery and intrigue might prefer the jungle effect created with ferns and moss and a miniature orchid. A tall bottle would suit best here.

If you are selecting your plants from nature, even if you don't know one plant from another you can observe carefully and then make selections. (See A Code for Good Green People, page 233.)

Look carefully at the surroundings. Look to see if the same plant is in various stages of growth. A plant just emerging won't tell you what its size will be. Look around at its neighbors to see if more mature plants will offer clues to size.

The *shape* of your container will determine which plants will look best and do well in it. If you have a squat decanter or are using a cheese dome, then you'll obviously want low-growing types of plants.

With tall bottles you can accommodate taller plants, but you will also want to tuck some shorter, fuller specimens into the arrangement to keep the tall fellow from looking lost and lonely.

Choose not only plants but other parts of the outdoors as well—small stones, twigs, nuts, etc. Kids love this sort of collecting, getting down close to the earth and actually looking at all the woodsy things available. A small, interesting rock or two, a twig bent in an unusual shape, a small weathered piece of branch, a bit of moss, shells from the beach.

Sophisticated, grown-up gardeners may not care for little ceramic frogs and such, but most children adore these too. So if you should spot a nice little green china frog in the dime store, or a fat brown clay toad or turtle, let the children add these to their collectibles.

The maintenance of a terrarium is chiefly a matter of watching out for too muches:

Too much water. When water collects on the inside of the glass—condensation—take off the cover for a few hours. Take a close look every month or so to see if the soil looks dry. (It's a good clue if moisture has not formed on the glass within a week or two.) Water can then be added, but sparingly. Do *not* overwater.

Too much growth. Prune when the plants seem to be growing out of bounds. Reach in to snip off dead leaves, too.

Too much fertilizer. Only a pinch in the water on infrequent occasions.

Too much light. No direct sun for long periods in the middle of the day. Plants won't be able to take the heat. Early morning and late afternoon sun, however, benefit flowering plants, such as the African violet and orchid. Some observation on your part will help you decide the best spot in the house for the terrarium collection—a place where it can be seen and enjoyed and where it receives at least enough light to maintain healthy-looking green leaves.

7 *Sharing the Designs in Nature*

To see a World in a Grain of Sand,
And a Heaven in a Wild Flower,
Hold Infinity in the palm of your hand,
And Eternity in an hour.
         —William Blake,
      "Auguries of Innocence"

    Anyone who has gardened for even a single season discovers with delight a whole world of enormously complex designs in nature. Designs that not only enthrall the mind and heart but charm the eye.

    Countless patterns are there for you to share when you look for the detail in your garden and beyond. The intricate veining in a leaf; the clear, certain architecture in a bird's nest; the moist, shining beauty of a melon split in half.

    Children need no urging at all to bring designs from nature into their lives. Smooth, flat rocks; graceful, fluted shells; an infinite variety of seed pods and packages—all are instantly recognizable as treasures to a child. But this natural delight in designs found in nature fairly blooms when he has someone with whom to share, search out and enjoy new treasures.

BEYOND THE GARDEN

Spore Prints—Mushroom Magic

Take the mushroom. A marvelous creation. It is not there one day, and the next day it is. Mushrooms can pop up overnight in your lawn, by a walkway in the park or in the woods.

Wherever you spot a mushroom growing, be sure to stop and take a careful look at it. The fluted undersides; the graceful, curving, ripply top; the strange, beautiful colors—all are worth several good long looks any day.

There are lots of different kinds of mushrooms, and they are all beautiful, some in strange, weird shapes and colors. Do *not* eat any of them. Some can be extremely poisonous. You want to grow up green all right—but that means a green heart and a green mind, not a green stomach.

Here is a fun way to capture a part of the mushroom's beauty for your designs from nature. Choose a mushroom with a wide umbrella top and pick it off low on the stem. (After you read the Code for Good Green People, page 233, you may want to choose several fresh-looking mushrooms from the supermarket instead of picking a particular wild one.)

At home, mix a small amount of water with just a bit of glue, thinning the glue enough so that you can spread it out over a piece of mounting paper with a brush wherever you want your design to be and only a bit larger than the diameter of the mushroom.

Cut off the stem of the mushroom, or else work it gently round and round with your fingers until it separates from the cap. If the mushroom's rim curves under to hide a good part of the fluted underpart, then carefully trim the rim away so that the spores will have a free fall to the paper.

Place the cap, underside down, over the paper and prop it up at the very, very edges with a couple of pencils so that the fluted underedge does not touch the paper.

Then turn a bowl over the cap and leave it for at least twenty-four hours. Now remove the bowl, and lift the mushroom cap ever so gently away. There on the paper will be a lovely design—made by the thousands of spores that fell from the underside of the mushroom cap.

The glue should be dry by this time and will hold the spores in place. You can then spray the print with hair lacquer to preserve the design.

Spider Webs

Now, these are really neat things. Their design is beautiful, and if you are lucky enough to come across one, see if you can't get hold of it to add to your collection of designs from nature.

(If you have read E. B. White's enchanting book *Charlotte's Web,* you might want to check first to see if the web you have found has a message written in it!)

One of the difficulties with collecting spider webs is that you never know when you're going to come across one, and you're not likely to have with you the things you need to get it home intact. Of course, you might let one of the darker corners of the living-room ceiling go untouched for a couple of years, but even at that, the best kinds of webs are the good, sturdy ones that are spun out of doors. Like Charlotte's.

So what you will most likely have to do when you do see a web that looks collectible is to beat it back home for the supplies, which amount to a spray can of enamel—black, say, if you want to mount it on white paper, or white if you want to mount it on black paper—and some old newspapers to put up to protect whatever, if anything, might be in the path in front of and behind you and the spider web.

Because what you'll do is stand about 3 or 4 feet away from the web—far enough away so that it won't be damaged from the pressure of the paint—and spray the web with enamel from both sides. Be careful not to overdo with the paint or the web will get too heavy and sag. Most spray enamels are fast-drying and you won't have to wait long for the web to be stiff enough to be cut at its guy lines and taken down carefully and mounted on your paper. The paint will still be tacky, so don't put anything on top of it.

While a black web outlined on white looks really great, if you happen to have a spider-web lover in your house who wants to spray the web he or she finds with pink enamel and put it on a lavender background, no one else is supposed to say, "Oh, no, it will look more like a spider web if it's black on white or white on black." You let the web collector become the proud owner of a pink web mounted against a lavender background.

Later on, this same web collector might want to try clear lacquer, which makes the neatest, most natural-looking web of all. Hung on a weathered board it is creepy-looking enough for those kids who get the greatest delight from spooky-looking things—kids about the ages of eight to fourteen.

spray paint from 3 ft. away

Fruit, Vegetable and Seed Prints

A whole range of truly distinctive designs can be made from ink prints of fruits, vegetables or seed pods. Citrus fruits make especially nice ink prints, suitable for stationery or framing. Use a sharp knife to slice these through the center crosswise. If you use vegetables such as green peppers, carrots or green beans, slice them through the center lengthwise. Do not remove any seeds or fibrous material, as these will add a lot of interest to the print.

Next, you need to prepare a big stamp pad. An ordinary stamp pad would work fine but most of them are not large enough. No matter. You can make your own.

Place several thicknesses of paper toweling in a pie pan or an aluminum tray such as those that bakery sweet rolls are often packaged in. Saturate the paper towels with waterproof drawing ink.

Now place the fruit or vegetable cut-side down on the "stamp pad" and press down lightly and uniformly. Then lift off and apply to your paper. Use a paper with a slightly absorbent texture rather than a slick-surface paper. Test out the print on an ordinary newspaper or on a school tablet before printing on your stationery paper.

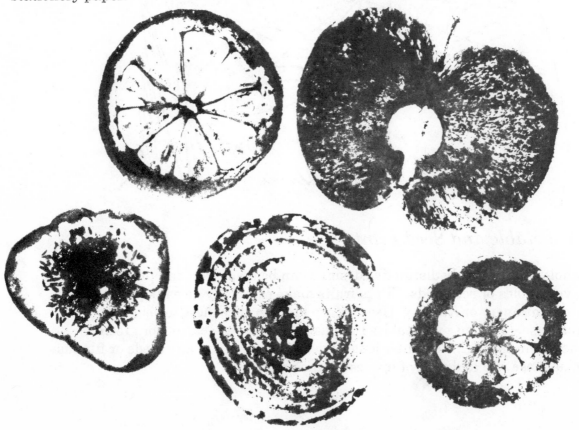

A little practice will enable you to make sharp, well-defined prints. Then you can have fun seeing all the beautiful and way-out designs you can get with different kinds of fruits and vegetables. How about a crosscut section of cabbage? An apple? A melon? Carve out a design in relief (one that sticks up from the surface) on half a potato and print with that. Slice a hyacinth bulb in half (can you bear it?), look first and marvel at the complete miniature flower that is hidden within the bulb, and then make a really super, smashing print with it.

Dandelion and Goatsbeard

Watch for a dandelion at the peak of its seed-bearing stage when the top is a loose, light ball of fluff. Some grow to a diameter of almost 2 inches, but the usual size is about 1 inch or 1½ inches.

Choose the largest you can find and pick it with as long a stem as possible. Pick carefully so that the seeds don't scatter from the head. Choose a still day if possible so that the wind won't scatter them either. You can also spray them lightly with hair spray before picking. And if you are very conservative (cautious), you can pick them just before the seed pods open and hang them in a cool place indoors. Then when the seed pods open, they will be protected from the wind and the birds, who truly love to eat them.

All right. So now you have a perfectly intact dandelion seed top and stem. Select a favorite color enamel and spray the dandelion top, rotating the stem of the plant as you spray. Hold your spray arm back away from the plant; wear an old plastic glove on the hand holding the dandelion; don't spray too much; and watch where you aim! It will take only seconds to color the dandelion (color the stem, too), and you will be amazed at the result—an intricate, delicate pattern in a beautiful color.

Pretty as dandelions can become with this treatment, goatsbeard can be even more spectacular. This is a wildflower, or weed if you will, native to Europe but now common along American roadsides. It resembles a dandelion but bears much larger blooms and correspondingly larger seed heads.

The fluffy, grayish-white balls are generally 2½ to 3 inches in diameter and 4-inch heads are not uncommon. These heads need to be harvested with the same special care as the dandelion's—hair spray before picking and careful transport home. (Try inserting stems upright in a bucket of sand.) When sprayed with pastel enamel, the heads reveal seed-pattern designs even more elaborate and striking than those of the dandelion. The finished seed heads are incomparable as a flower arrangement by themselves or as an accent in companion arrangements. With care, they will last at least two years.

Stump Rubbings

No matter what the reason, it is truly sad to see a tree cut down. Too often, a tree just happens to be in a place where someone, somewhere, determines that something else should be.

The cutting of trees is necessary many times, of course. For the building materials we need and the space for homes built from them. Or sometimes a tree sickens and dies. In public parks and on city streets, trees that are obviously and hopelessly ailing are usually taken down immediately.

Well, sad though it be, should you come across a tree newly taken down and the stump is still there, you've got a good chance to make a stump rubbing.

You'll need paper large enough to stretch across the stump from one side to the other and a bit down the sides so that you can thumbtack it in place. Shelf paper is good. Some types of computer read-out paper also come in long strips, so don't overlook that idea if you happen to have an in with a computer.

For all except the biggest of trees, though, you ought to try to get hold of a big size of artist's sketch paper (at any art-supply store).

Whatever paper you use, stretch it across the stump and thumbtack it securely on both sides and around the sides as needed to keep it well in place. Lay a piece of charcoal (which gives a great rubbing, as does a pastel, and you might prefer that) on its side and rub across the paper. Rub only in one direction—from one side straight across to the other.

210

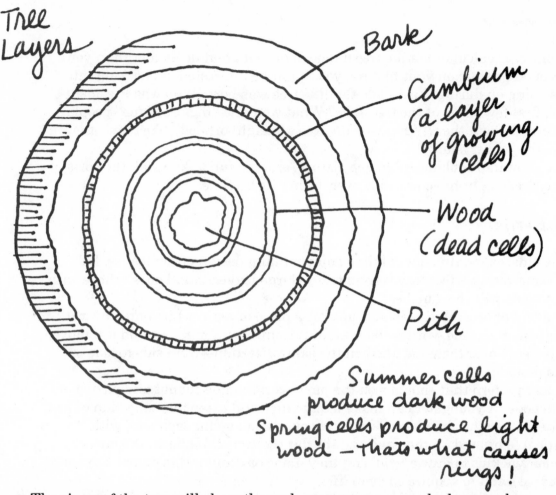

Tree Layers

Bark

Cambium (a layer of growing cells)

Wood (dead cells)

Pith

Summer cells produce dark wood
Spring cells produce light wood — that's what causes rings!

The rings of the tree will show through on your paper, and when you have finished you will have not only an attractive rubbing but a history of the tree right in your hands. The number of rings will tell you approximately how old the tree was. Subtract that number from the current year and you will know the approximate birth date of the tree. You will also know the years when the tree went thirsty from drought—the thinnest rings will tell you that. The years when there was lots of rain and the tree grew more—those were the years of the widest rings.

If from your calculations the tree happens to be a great deal older than you are, and you are not up on your history, you might be interested in checking into what was going on during the decade that the tree was born. Who was President during the first few years of the tree's life? What were the "big problems" people were concerned about then? What was the tree's "neighborhood" like then—the city, town, the countryside?

It's *your* stump rubbing, *your* tree history, and it's fun to know all the sorts of things your tree might have presided over during its lifetime.

Leaf Patterns

Little kids, especially, never fail to enjoy making designs from leaves. Let them gather several perfect leaves from trees—large leaves, small ones. Those with prominent veins will show up best.

Lay a leaf on the table, vein-side up. Put a piece of plain white paper over it. Turn a crayon on its side, with most or all of the paper wrapping around it removed, and rub it evenly over the paper. Rub in the same direction—from side to side or from up to down.

The leaf pattern that emerges on the paper can then be cut out and pasted on or in a notebook. A youngster can make a quite nice and extensive collection of leaf patterns to put together in a loose-leaf notebook. One page for each leaf, with the name of the tree printed on the page and the date collected. While on the latter point, encourage kids to date everything they make or design. It is a nice, tidy, and often valuable habit to acquire early in life.

The small leaf designs can be pasted onto any paper of choice and the paper used for notepaper and stationery.

Other designs from leaves can be made with paint prints. Choose a piece of paper with a soft-textured surface, not slick. Mimeograph paper works well. Paint the undersides of the leaves with poster paint. Use lots.

Now carefully place the paper over the leaf, centering it, before you put it down, where you want the print to appear. Then roll over the whole thing carefully,

212

carefully, with a rolling pin or smooth round bottle. (Have newspaper or something else expendable under the leaf in case your lots of paint turns out to be too much and oozes out. Should this happen, try again with lots of paint but not as much!)

Lift the paper off, and on the underneath side you will have a color reproduction of your leaf. Let dry and then label your print with the type of tree, date and where collected. Place inside a plastic envelope and keep in a loose-leaf notebook.

Children will also enjoy picking a leaf down to its bones to highlight the beautiful design in its framework. The resulting leaf skeletons can be used in flower arrangements, collages, and other ways as pressed flowers. They are especially attractive when combined with a few bleached seashells from the beach.

Leaves that have heavy veins and texture work best. Bring to a boil 2 quarts of water and 2 tablespoons of sal soda (a cleaning agent available at the grocery store). Add leaves and cook for a half hour. Let the water cool; drain the leaves; rinse gently with cold water; and drain again.

Place the leaves on a work surface (a kitchen cutting board is good) and with a soft toothbrush gently brush away the leaf parts, leaving only the skeletons: the stalks and veins. Easy does it.

After the leaf parts are removed, the skeletons can be bleached by putting them in a solution of 2 tablespoons of bleach to 1 quart of water and leaving them there for an hour. Pour off the solution and rinse the skeletons gently in cold water. The skeletons can also be tinted if you want (most children want) by putting them in a solution of water that has been deeply colored with food coloring. When they are tinted the shade desired, remove and blot them in paper toweling. Now you can arrange them on a flat surface (back to the old cutting board) in the shapes desired and press for at least a couple of days till dry. (See Pressing Flowers, page 223.)

IN A FLOWER

Not even the smallest of children needs to have the beauty of a flower pointed out to him. No florist's association or Mother's Day commercial need tell the toddler that a flower—any flower—makes a lovely gift.

One of the most enduring rituals of childhood (and fondest memories of parenthood) is the presentation of flowers that have been picked with delight and love. Whether a fistful of buttercups from a field, a single dandelion from the park or a bouquet chosen with the greatest of deliberation from a garden, the gift —and the bearer of it—tell all there is to know about the joys of sharing the designs in nature.

For these small but grand gifts from the young, a couple of special flower containers are worth having on hand. An empty cologne bottle, tall and slim, will handle a single brown-eyed Susan. A salt shaker—top left on and holes perhaps widened a bit with an ice pick—will prop up a drooping clump of Johnny-jump-ups. In such ways does the older heart sharpen its sense of what the younger eye has seen. And the small, unexpected flower gift claims its status on its own terms, not patronized in any way.

Other sources for vases or cachepots that children will enjoy making include coffee cans, frozen-juice containers, and cheese and margarine cartons. And all these lend themselves to painting, papering, decoupage, and all kinds of artsy-craftsy fun.

Groupings of small, narrow jars and bottles or test tubes (the latter found in laboratory-equipment stores if not in the remnants of a toy chemistry set), of varying heights and sizes, linked together with masking tape or glue, have special appeal for children.

Such holders are fun to assemble for a centerpiece—a favorite arrangement with children. If clear glass bottles are used, children will also like tinting the water with food coloring to help carry out their color scheme. (This is also known as gilding the lily, but there is no denying children like it.)

Flower Arranging

FOUR EASY-TO-REMEMBER DESIGNS

Some children seem to feel more confident in flower arranging if they can follow basic directions step by step. Others want such suggestions merely as a taking-off point for doing their own thing. Either way, a few basic designs can help open up a wider view of possibilities.

Three branches and a flower

You will need a shallow bowl and a flower holder. (A pinholder usually works best. Roll floral clay into a ball, press onto the bottom of the pinholder, and then press the pinholder into the bowl, close to one edge of the container.)

Cut three pieces of foliage for the basic triangle. You can use evergreen boughs or even bare branches. The length of the triangle pieces will depend on the size of your container.

Show your child how to measure with his hand. Spread your hand out. The span from your little finger to your thumb counts as one hand measure. Move your thumb over to mark the little finger's place, stretch the hand out again in inchworm fashion, and you have a measurement of two hands. If your child measures bowls and branches and stems in this way, he won't have to run for a ruler each time. Before long his eye will tell him proper proportions.

For the three-branches-and-a-flower arrangement, the tallest branch should be one and a half times the width of the container plus the height of the container. If your container measures two hands wide, for example, then your tallest branch should be three hands tall plus the height of the container.

Cut the next branch as long as the width of the container plus its height, and the third piece one half the width plus its height.

Arrange in the container as illustrated and add the flower, its stem an inch or so long, at the base of the tallest branch.

The saucer arrangement

Use leaves or branches to form the saucer. You will need perhaps nine leaves for the saucer, and three or five flowers for the center. Arrange as shown. Cut the center flower stems in different lengths so that the flowers will each be separate and not bunched together.

216

The reverse S

An English painter, William Hogarth, called this design "the line of beauty." The container for it must be taller than it is wide. Ferns are good to use to trace the design. One line curves up, the other curves down, to form a reverse S. Arrange several flower heads (an uneven number) close to the rim of the container to follow the curve. Arrange so that no two blossoms are at quite the same level.

Ikebana

Ikebana is an art that has been practiced by the Japanese for hundreds and hundreds of years. Only the most superficial sampling of this enormously detailed and beautiful way of arranging flowers can be presented here, though enough perhaps to interest you in learning more about *ikebana* and its tranquil philosophy that appeals as much to the spirit as to the eye.

1. *Ikebana* is based on the principle of three main lines in the design. These lines symbolize Heaven, Man and Earth.
2. Heaven is always the longest line. Earth, the base, is the shortest line. Man, the joining or reconciling line, is in between in length.
3. The flowers or branches representing Man and Earth are always placed so that the tips are turned toward Heaven.
4. In *ikebana,* the various kinds of flowers and branches have special significance, and certain kinds have special meanings for festivals and other occasions. The two colors red and white, for example, are used for happy occasions. White alone represents a sad occasion.
5. The special flower for boys is the iris; for girls, the peach.

There are several different categories of *ikebana,* and designs within each of these categories have varying requirements. Here are just two examples.

Seika is the name of a classical type of *ikebana.* Its formal style has very strict rules for placement of the plant material. In many ways such rules make it easier and more fun for a beginner to follow. *Seika* designs can, of course, be enormously intricate, too, with endless possibilities, because the arrangements can use three, five, seven or nine lines (always an uneven number), although the three basics are

217

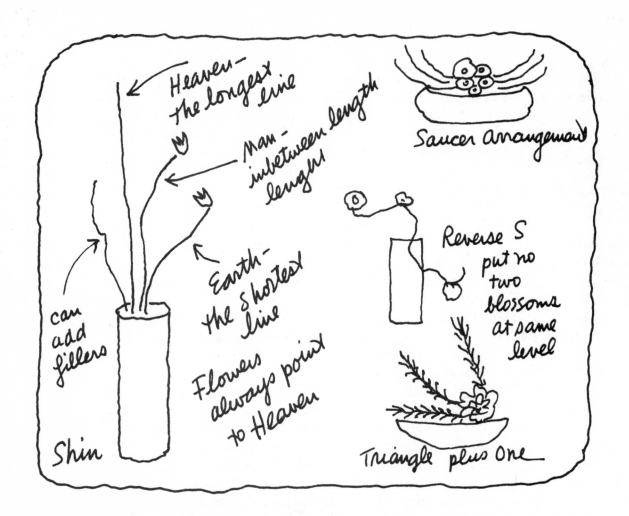

Heaven— the longest line

Man— inbetween length length

Earth— the shortest line

Flowers always point to Heaven

can add fillers

Shin

Saucer arrangement

Reverse S put no two blossoms at same level

Triangle plus One

still considered the main lines.

Rules for *seika* of the upright, or *shin,* style (illustrated) include:

1. The style is always tall and slender—container and arrangement. All stems must be placed so that they appear to be as one as they come up out of the container. (Which means they may need to be tied together;

218

the Japanese used small forked sticks concealed in the tall container to do the trick.)

2. No plant material can extend sideways beyond the width of the container.
3. The stems should be plain, no leaves or twigs left on, for a few inches above the rim of the container.
4. For this arrangement, the Heaven stem extends one and a half times the height of the container. However, if you are emphasizing the height of a flower such as the gladiola, then the tallest stem, Heaven, might be three times the height of the container.
5. The length of Man is two-thirds that of Heaven.
6. The length of Earth is one-third that of Heaven.

The slanting, or *moribana,* style is a more naturalistic design which duplicates the natural pattern of growth. With *moribana* you can use your own imagination while remembering these guidelines.

1. In general, the length of the Heaven stem should be at least as long as the width plus the height of the container. Or it may measure two times the width of the container.
2. The plant and the container must be considered together to help you decide the arrangement.
3. The larger the plant you have, the larger the container you will need.
4. If you are using thick and sturdy branches, they can be cut shorter.
5. A heavy, thick container can support a taller design in *moribana* than can a thin, fragile container.
6. Whatever Heaven's measure, the length of Man will be three-quarters that of Heaven, and Earth's measurement will be three-quarters the length of Man.
7. Flowers, leaves, moss or such are used at the base of the arrangement to conceal the stems and also the holder (usually a pin type anchored with floral clay).

MINIATURE ARRANGEMENTS

Of special fun for children are arrangements made up of the tiniest sorts of flowers. These are the blooms children seem to spot much easier than adults:

Johnny-jump-ups, chickweed, clover, buttercups.

For these arrangements, children can collect their own vases too: small bottles, the screw tops of other bottles, the fancy cases of used-up lipsticks, the tiny bottles often sold in import stores. If they simply think tiny container, they will come up with other ideas of their own. Small bits of floral Oasis can be used to help keep one flower upright and in place. Wet sand will work, too.

Such tiny arrangements will find an appreciative audience when placed on a desk or bureau top, especially if a magnifying glass is kept near by. Obviously, fresh flowers are also well received by dollhouse inhabitants.

It's a good idea to keep together in one place the few things you'll need to make flower arranging easy and fun. A small tool kit, tackle box, sewing box, plastic household-cleaning caddy—any of these will be more than large enough to help you keep your flower things organized. These include scissors, florist's clay, pinholders, other frogs (marbles and such), Oasis, containers for the small, spur-of-the-moment flower offering. Also keep on hand a roll of florist's wire for the droopy flower that will not hold its head where you want it or the flower in need of first-aid treatment for a broken stem. Children will love tending to these needs. Here's how.

Flowers with a hollow stem: Cut a piece of wire an inch longer than the length of the stem. Run the wire up through the bottom of the stem until the tip touches the base of the flower. Now push very gently just until the wire enters the bloom. Stop! Snip off any wire that extends below the stem. Your flower can now be bent to whatever curve you wish, and its head will stay where it is put, too.

Flowers with a nonhollow stem: Cut a piece of wire several inches longer than the stem. (The actual length of wire needed will depend on how long and how thick the stem is—you will soon be able to judge accurately.)

Hold the flower gently with one hand, fingers under the base of the bloom, and with the other hand push the wire carefully into the stem just below the base of the bloom. Now hold that end of the wire in place with one hand while you wrap the rest of the wire gently around the stem, spacing the wire an inch or so apart as it encircles the stem (this will depend on the limpness of the stem), and snip the wire off at the base.

SOME OTHER THINGS TO KNOW IN TREATING
CUT FLOWERS KINDLY

1. Use sharp scissors. A purist might prefer a sharp knife for making the cleanest cut without squnching the stems, but obviously sharp knives are risky in the hands of a young child. A pair of good sharp scissors—preferably kept for flower cutting only—will do the job.

2. Cut stems on the slant. Here the purists may differ. Some prefer a slant cut; others say it makes no difference. The slant cut does expose more of the stem to the water; does keep it from standing flat on the bottom of the vase or holder; and therefore it can allow the stem to take up more water. Besides, cutting on the slant adds a bit of special mystique to flower cutting, and kids like that.

3. Put flowers into water right after cutting. Some experts say hot water; some say ice water. So why not operate on the theory that an unsuspecting flower won't appreciate the shock of one extreme or the other any more than most people would. Put your flowers in a deep pitcher of faintly cool water.

4. Take off all leaves that will be underwater when the flowers are arranged. *No* one disagrees about this. Leaves left on underwater will rot quickly and the water will smell terrible.

5. Add fresh water every day.

6. Keep arrangement away from direct sun, radiators, drafts.

7. To keep cut flowers fresh longer, all kinds of treatments have been suggested, debated, and sometimes debunked. A number are listed below. You might want to experiment with some of these ideas and see if you can detect which, if any, seem to prolong the life of your cut flowers.

   An aspirin dissolved in the water.

   A teaspoon of sugar stirred into the water.

   A nail placed in the bottom of the container.

A relatively new suggestion, from horticulturists at Michigan State University: to make a quart of solution, mix 1 pint of water with 1 pint of a carbonated soft drink containing citric acid—Sprite or 7Up, for example. Add ½ teaspoon of chlorine bleach and stir well before using. Commercial preservatives used by florists can increase the life of cut flowers considerably and can be obtained from some florists' shops and supply houses.

PRESSING FLOWERS

Beautiful designs can also be made from pressed flowers and other plant material. The plant press can be nothing more pretentious than a fat telephone book or a thick stack of newspapers. A young collector, however, will enjoy making a special plant press.

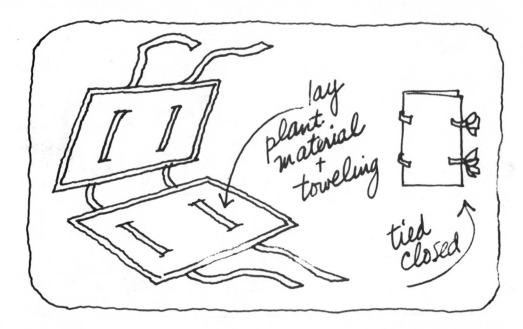

lay plant material + toweling

tied closed

You will need two pieces of heavy-weight cardboard. You can cut out two sides of a cardboard carton to get the pieces you need. About 12 by 14 inches is a good size for a beginner press—small enough for a youngster to tote along easily and big enough for most of the plant materials he will want to press. It is of such a size, too, that he will be able to fill his press and consider that he has found a sufficient amount on the collecting jaunt and still not have scooped up a great deal more plant material than he can possibly handle.

Put masking tape around the corrugated edges to prevent tearing and to give a finished look to the press. Make a slit in each piece of cardboard at each of the corners, about 2 inches in from the sides. Thread about 1-inch-wide ribbon (grosgrain is a good choice—pretty, sturdy and easy to tie and untie) through the slits. Leave 3 or 4 inches of ribbon in between the two pieces and about 8 inches on each end for tying. Altogether, two strips of ribbon, each about a yard long, should do the trick.

224

You'll also be using paper toweling or newspaper for soaking up the moisture in the plants while they are being pressed flat. Paper toweling is much nicer to work with than newspaper, and not all that expensive. (Choose a kind that is smooth—without a waffle or other embossed design on it, else your pressings will wind up waffled, too.) The size of a regular toweling sheet is about 11 by 11 inches, so will fit the 12-by-14 press nicely. Have a number of layers of toweling, or newspaper, in your press and ready to use when you set out collecting.

If you are making a special jaunt out to do collecting, which can be a fun occasion in itself, choose a dry, sunny day—midmorning to midafternoon. Wet weather means wet plants that won't dry out quickly. Early morning is not such a good time because the dew that is still on the plants can mean longer drying time, too.

Don't *pick* the flowers or other plant specimens. Cut with a sharp pair of scissors. Look for all kinds of plant material, not just flowers: leaves, weeds, grasses, fronds and stems.

As you choose the plant material, arrange each piece on a layer of toweling (about four sheets thick) and far enough apart so that the specimens don't touch each other. Watch to see that you don't have thick and thin sorts of plants on the same sheet of toweling, else they won't press equally flat.

When the first toweling layer is filled, place another layer on top of it (three or four sheets) and then start a new layer of pressings. Continue building layers in this way, putting four sheets of toweling on the top of the last collection and then tieing your press together.

At home, lay the press flat and weight it down—under a heavy pile of books or at the very bottom of a big stack of magazines. Wait at least three or four days, then take the press out and go through carefully, replacing the towels layer by layer with new pieces. Then tie the whole thing back up and put under the weight again for another three days (at least) to be certain the plants are really dry.

If you have selected flowers with a thick center for pressing—a daisy, say, or a brown-eyed Susan—then separate the petals and leaves from the stems and centers and press separately. When put together again in an arrangement, you would never know that they had ever been separated.

If your flowers seem to have faded after pressing, you can perk up their looks with watercolor paints. Children of all ages love this bit of refurbishing. Leave the flower lying flat while you paint it and handle as little as possible. Use a very fine, sable watercolor brush.

If you find you are having difficulty getting the color to stick to the petal, dip your brush lightly into a bit of mild dishwashing detergent before dipping into the watercolor.

To anchor your plant materials in an arrangement, put a tiny spot of glue on the back of each piece—use the point of a toothpick. Spread the glue gently around a bit and put the plant piece into place. Smaller children enjoy making their arrangements on construction paper first—of a color that will blend with the final background of the arrangement. After each flower, stem and so on is anchored to the construction paper, it can be handled much easier. The child can then cut out around each part of the arrangement to transfer it to its final spot—whether a book cover, picture or tray.

As for places to use your pressed plants, the cover of your own press book would be a good place to start. Arrange the plant material as you choose and tack temporarily with a tiny bit of glue underneath. You can cover it in any number of ways. For example, sheets of plastic with adhesive backing make a very durable covering, but can be tricky for a small child to manage (let's face it—adults, too) because once the plastic sheet catches on, it catches on. There is no loosening, straightening out, rescuing plant material from the clutches of the adhesive to rearrange it. The moment of truth is there when the adhesive backing touches down.

A clear plastic spray can also be used. All children seem to go for spray-can action, and all of them tend to overdo it. So a "That's enough" will likely be in order here. You need to tack down the material firmly all around the edges first, and then just a thin film from the plastic spray. After the spray is dry, for extra durability you can brush on several coats of clear, nonyellowing shellac, letting each coat dry thoroughly in between.

For mounting on boards or trays, or the sides of cans (which can then make nice flower vases and cachepots), spray the object with lacquer. Let it dry, then buff up a bit with a very fine sandpaper. Spray again and then arrange the plant material while the lacquer is still wet. Use your watercolor brush to scootch the plant material about as you want it (preplanned so you don't lose too much time—lacquer dries fast) and press gently into place. When dry, spray the whole thing again.

One of the most practical and most attractive places for pressed flowers and other plant material is in a picture arrangement. The frames—glass, backing and all—can be purchased inexpensively at the dime store unless you happen to have an extra on hand. Choose the frame first, though, and then fit the arrangement to it. Don't arrange on a piece of cardboard or mounting paper and then have to look and search for something to fit those special dimensions. It can delay the finish of the project needlessly.

FLOWERS IN ART

You will find that only a few sessions of flower designing can be sufficiently consciousness-raising to make any visit to an art gallery much more enjoyable for children. Still lifes abound in many collections. And once an awareness of nature becomes such a tangible part of your children's lives, all expressions of man's relationship to nature take on new meanings for them—including still lifes and landscapes. Both you and your children will look at the artists' efforts more intently. The design will mean more. The cubist still lifes of Georges Braque, the mysterious jungles of Rousseau, can virtually come alive for a child, stretching his world far beyond its geographic limits.

Your child may enjoy setting up a still-life design of his own at home for painting. Encourage him to use the flowers and vegetables he has grown himself, arranged as he chooses.

If inexpensive reproductions are available, as they are from many museums, your child might also enjoy setting up a still life like one of the masters' and then

putting to paper or canvas his own interpretation of the scene.

If an art gallery or museum is not within reach for a personal visit, then send for the Catalog of Reproductions that is available free from the National Gallery of Art (write to Publications Fund, National Gallery of Art, Washington, D.C. 20565). In this catalog, you will find a number of still-life reproductions offered in postcard size for 10 cents apiece. The price is hard to beat for a view of Cézanne's "Vase of Flowers," Matisse's "Pot of Geraniums," Braque's "Peonies."

ON A STARRY NIGHT

Having begun this book with a Beautiful Day, where else to end but with a Starry Night—the grandest design of all. Stargazing for real is free to everyone. If you live in the city, be sure to take advantage of the chance to look at the heavens on those nights when smog isn't hovering over everything. And remember, winter skies have the brightest constellations.

For indoor fun, and a neat way to preface going to sleep, a youngster can build his own planetarium. All he will need is a flashlight and an oatmeal carton and some cardboard.

Start with the carton. Cut out a circle in the bottom end, leaving a quarter-inch rim. Put masking tape around the cut edges of the rim to reinforce. Now, stand the box on a piece of cardboard and trace circles with a pencil. Cut out these circles—on the *inside* of the line so that they will be just a bit smaller than the carton and will slip down inside to make a new bottom resting against the inside of the rim.

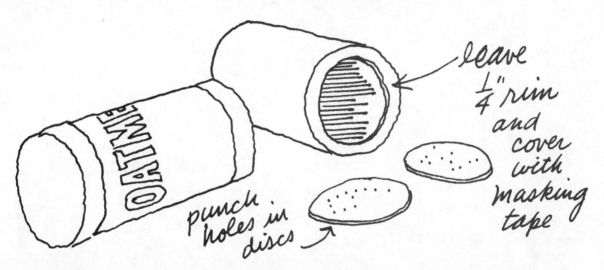

On each circle, mark out the stars for a different constellation—the Big Dipper; Orion, the mighty hunter; the Northern Cross; Hydra, the sea serpent. With an ice pick, nut pick or such, punch out small, neat holes where you have the stars marked. Then all that is left for the stargazer to do is wait around until bedtime.

Now he can put a constellation card into the carton, push it down snugly to the bottom, turn out the lights, hop into bed, turn on his flashlight, put it up inside the carton and point toward the ceiling. There is his own starry sky!

231

PART THREE APPENDICES

A CODE FOR GOOD GREEN PEOPLE

A good green person knows what things from nature can be collected and what cannot.

Nice people, smart people, good green people, do not gather plant materials willy-nilly out of public parks or off of other people's property. They do not rip plants out by their roots, or trample or injure other growing things. And they do not gather a whole lot more plant material than they can use.

They know the laws that their state may have to protect certain types of wildflowers and other plants. They know that in protected areas—a refuge, a national forest, a state park—they do not pick up and take off so much as a rock or a twig. These are places to visit, to reverence, to leave as they are. And nowhere do they stuff their pockets, their duffel bags, their food coolers with nature's belongings.

They ask permission if they venture onto private woodlands or meadows. They know when it's okay to scrounge on the vacant lot or down by the creek— when Queen Anne's lace or milkweed pods or pine cones, acorns, berries, sycamore balls, hickory nuts, or Osage oranges abound and collecting a few will not be destructive at all.

They know enough not to lay waste the last few flowers of a kind or dig up the only plant specimen of its kind that may be growing in the vicinity. They learned in the very first stages of growing green a rhyme that flits in their heads whenever they might be collecting from nature:

> If of this plant you don't see many,
> Then be a good guy and don't pick any.

Good green people also recognize that there are times and places where collecting plants is not only sensible but advisable—on roadsides about to be bulldozed and on land about to be cleared for housing tracts, apartments, highrises. Rescuing what plant life can be saved here is only balancing off the idiocy with which much of it is being destroyed in the first place. When a green good guy comes up against the workings of a wall-to-wall asphalt mind, he ought to feel free to salvage whatever he can from the encounter.

Good green people also know that in walks through city streets and parks, what blows off the trees can be fair collecting material. A perfect leaf specimen or seed pod is certainly all right for picking up from the grass or sidewalk and carefully carrying home to preserve.

Actually, all that the code for good green people means is that while you are enjoying and learning all you can about green and growing things, you take special pains to make sure you have done nothing to diminish the enjoyment of all the other green people who will follow you. And in a positive way, you enhance and replenish and replace wherever you have the opportunity to do so.

ENDANGERED PLANT SPECIES

    Most people are aware of endangered species in the animal world. Now more people need to know that there are endangered species in the plant world, too. About two thousand major plant species are in danger of disappearing altogether.

    Some are threatened by disease: lethal yellowing is killing the coconut palm in

southern Florida, and thousands of America's most beautiful city trees have been lost to Dutch elm disease, spread by the elm bark beetle. Whole streets that were once graceful green archways have been laid bare by this destructive pest. (We know about the balance of nature, the rights of all living things to a place in the scheme of things, the intricate relationships with which a whole ecosystem survives, but despite all this, it is hard not to hate the bark beetle for destroying so many of our beautiful American elms.)

Many wildflowers along roadsides cannot survive years of automobile exhaust fumes (and it is not hard at all to hate the automobile!). But most plants, as with animals, are endangered simply by man crowding them out of their native environments.

When a swamp or marsh is drained and filled or when a woodland is cleared, plants that may have grown only in that particular place are gone forever. Even now, some plants, like some animals, are so rare that they can be seen only in zoos. (A plant zoo is listed in your phone book as a botanical garden.)

Perhaps there is an area in or near your community which you would like to see kept in its natural state. Local garden and conservation clubs may already be working on such a project. You and your friends can help by contributing money to such a project or by helping to keep such an area litter-free. If you aren't certain how to get in touch with a group interested in preserving our environment, you can send for a pamphlet titled *Groups That Can Help; A Directory of Environmental Organizations*. It costs 15 cents, purchased from the Superintendent of Documents, U. S. Government Printing Office, Washington, D. C. 20402.

STATE FLOWERS, BIRDS, TREES

State	Flower	Bird	Tree
ALABAMA	Camellia	Yellowhammer	Southern (Longleaf) Pine
ALASKA	Forget-me-not	Willow Ptarmigan	Sitka Spruce
ARIZONA	Giant Cactus, or Saguaro	Cactus Wren	Paloverde
ARKANSAS	Apple Blossom	Mockingbird	Pine
CALIFORNIA	California Poppy	Valley Quail	Redwood
COLORADO	Columbine	Lark Bunting	Colorado Blue Spruce
CONNECTICUT	Mountain Laurel	American Robin	White Oak
DELAWARE	Peach Blossom	Blue Hen Chicken	American Holly
FLORIDA	Orange Blossom	Mockingbird	Sabal Palm
GEORGIA	Cherokee Rose	Brown Thrasher	Live Oak
HAWAII	Hibiscus	Nene (Hawaiian Goose)	Kukui (Candlenut)
IDAHO	Lewis Mock Orange	Mountain Bluebird	Western White Pine
ILLINOIS	Native Violet	Cardinal	Bur Oak
INDIANA	Peony	Cardinal	Tulip (Yellow Poplar)
IOWA	Wild Rose	Eastern Goldfinch	Oak
KANSAS	Sunflower	Western Meadowlark	Cottonwood
KENTUCKY	Goldenrod	Cardinal	Tulip Tree
LOUISIANA	Southern Magnolia	Eastern Brown Pelican	Bald Cypress
MAINE	Pine Cone and Tassel	Chickadee	Eastern White Pine
MARYLAND	Black-eyed Susan	Baltimore Oriole	White Oak
MASSACHUSETTS	Mayflower	Chickadee	American Elm
MICHIGAN	Apple Blossom	Robin	White Pine
MINNESOTA	Showy Lady's-slipper	Loon	Red (Norway) Pine
MISSISSIPPI	Magnolia	Mockingbird	Magnolia
MISSOURI	Hawthorn	Eastern Bluebird	Dogwood

State	Flower	Bird	Tree
MONTANA	Bitterroot	Western Meadowlark	Ponderosa Pine
NEBRASKA	Goldenrod	Western Meadowlark	American Elm
NEVADA	Sagebrush	Mountain Bluebird	Single-leaf Piñon
NEW HAMPSHIRE	Purple Lilac	Purple Finch	Paper (White) Birch
NEW JERSEY	Purple Violet	Eastern Goldfinch	Red Oak
NEW MEXICO	Yucca	Road Runner	Piñon (Nut Pine)
NEW YORK	Rose	Bluebird	Sugar Maple
NORTH CAROLINA	Dogwood	Cardinal	Pine
NORTH DAKOTA	Wild Prairie Rose	Western Meadowlark	American Elm
OKLAHOMA	Mistletoe	Scissor-tailed Flycatcher	Redbud
OREGON	Oregon Grape	Western Meadowlark	Douglas Fir
PENNSYLVANIA	Mountain Laurel	Ruffed Grouse	Eastern Hemlock
RHODE ISLAND	Violet	Rhode Island Red	Red Maple
SOUTH CAROLINA	Carolina (Yellow) Jessamine	Carolina Wren	Palmetto
SOUTH DAKOTA	American Pasque	Ring-necked Pheasant	Black Hills Spruce
TENNESSEE	Iris	Mockingbird	Tulip Poplar
TEXAS	Bluebonnet	Mockingbird	Pecan
UTAH	Sego Lily	California Gull	Blue Spruce
VERMONT	Red Clover	Hermit Thrush	Sugar Maple
VIRGINIA	Flowering Dogwood	Cardinal	Flowering Dogwood
WASHINGTON	Coast Rhododendron	American Goldfinch	Western Hemlock
WEST VIRGINIA	Rhododendron Maximum	Cardinal	Sugar Maple
WISCONSIN	Butterfly Violet	Robin	Sugar Maple
WYOMING	Wyoming Paint Brush	Western Meadowlark	Plains Cottonwood (Balsam Poplar)
DISTRICT OF COLUMBIA	American Beauty Rose	Wood Thrush	Scarlet Oak

HORTICULTURAL SOCIETIES

Clubs have special appeal for young people, and what could be more special than membership in a society devoted to a part of the green world in which you have a special interest? Most of the organizations listed below publish magazines or newsletters and all would welcome inquiries about membership. Just because you're still growing green doesn't mean you won't be welcomed heartily . . . and age limits don't apply. As a matter of fact, the gloxinia society listed below was founded by Elvin McDonald, now garden editor of *House Beautiful* magazine, when he was thirteen years old!

African Violet Society of America
P.O. Box 1326
Knoxville, Tenn. 37901

American Amaryllis Society
2678 Prestwick Ct.
La Jolla, Ca. 92037

American Begonia Society
530 S. Barnett Lane
Anaheim, Ca. 92805

Bromeliad Society
647 South Saltair Ave.
Los Angeles, Ca. 90049

Cactus and Succulent Society of America
2631 Fairgreen Ave.
Arcadia, Ca. 91006

American Daffodil Society
10 Othoridge Rd.
Lutherville, Md. 21093

American Fern Society
c/o Robert Stolze
Field Museum
Chicago, Ill. 60605

International Geranium Society
2547 Blvd. Del Campo
San Luis Obispo, Ca. 93401

American Gloxinia and Gesneriad Society
58 Hill Street
Tewksbury, Mass. 01876

American Gourd Society
Mr. John Stevens
Box 274, RR 1
Mt. Gilead, Oh. 43338

Herb Society of America Horticultural Hall
300 Massachusetts Ave.
Boston, Mass. 02115

American Horticultural Society
Mount Vernon, Va. 22121

American Society for Horticultural Science
P.O. Box 109 914 Main Street
St. Joseph, Mich. 49085

Ikebana International, N. Y. Chapter
333 East 47th St.
New York, N.Y. 10017

International Shade Tree Conference
P.O. Box 71
3 Lincoln Square
Urbana, Ill. 61801

American Plant Life Society
2678 Prestwick Ct.
La Jolla, Ca. 92037